With love & gratitude for all you have done for so many children
love Charlie x

100 Little Words on Parenthood

As told by parents, grandparents and experts

GW00634576

Compiled by Charlie Plunkett

www.charlieplunkett.co.uk

**Grosvenor House
Publishing Limited**

Charlie Plunkett is hereby identified as author of this
work in accordance with Section 77 of the Copyright, Designs
and Patents Act 1988

The book cover picture is copyright to Charlie Plunkett

This book is published by
Grosvenor House Publishing Ltd
28-30 High Street, Guildford, Surrey, GU1 3EL.
www.grosvenorhousepublishing.co.uk

A CIP record for this book
is available from the British Library

ISBN 978-1-78148-162-2

Also by Charlie Plunkett

The True Diary of a Bride-to-be

The True Diary of a Mum-to-be:
a pregnancy companion

The True Diary of Baby's First Year:
a mothering companion

Coming soon...
The Toddler Files

What parents are saying about...

100 Little Words on Parenthood

'Gorgeous book, love it. Great little anecdotes and laugh out loud moments. Amazing how just 100 words can also make you cry the minute after you were just laughing...'

'What a marvellous little book about parenthood ... heart-warming, wonderful and happy ... well observed and really a lovely collection ...'

'100 little words is a little treasure, perfectly complemented by the little truisms and quotations interspersed between each contributor's special memory. A joy to read, a delightful gift.'

'I feel this could be great for new parents for a fun and intriguing read to see the enjoyment others have experienced. Yes; put away those guide books and get this!'

'A beautiful collection of thoughts and anecdotes that makes you smile, laugh and shed a tear. Very well collated and a joy to read...'

'When I was pregnant I read everything I could about pregnancy and parenting. Most books went into great detail. But 100 Little Words on Parenthood gives you all the best bits cut down into 100 word snippets. It makes you laugh, it makes you cry, but most of all as a parent it makes you realise you're not alone!'

'A really nice collection of poems, anecdotes, true stories and helpful tips about babies, kids and parenting. Touching, informative and amusing too.'

'A beautiful, poignant and funny collection. Thank you Charlie for creating such a magical little book.'

'100 Little Words is an insightful collection of accounts of parenthood from the front line. Covering every aspect from birth to becoming a grandparent Charlie has managed to pull together a rich variety of writers to contribute to this masterful collection of parental reflections. It's genuinely funny, often heart-breaking and always honest. Any parent would be wise to purchase this to gain insight into the often bewildering world of parenthood.'

Acknowledgements

To everyone who has helped me with this book I am extremely grateful for your time and for allowing us a glimpse into your life.

In particular I must thank the very creative and lovely Bryan Hamilton, designer of my beautiful cover and ebook formatter. (www.ekindle.co.uk)

Dedication

I would like to dedicate this book to my parents and to all of you mums, dads and grandparents out there. You are unsung heroes, the glue that holds this world together.

Contents

100 Little Words on Parenthood

Introduction

The idea for this book came about whilst I was working on a new parenting book called The Toddler Files. I had just become a Twitter convert and, for someone who struggles to condense words, was finding it a challenge to keep my tweets within the 140 characters. As I started writing about my little boy's escapades, from his first birthday through to his first day at school, I pondered on whether it was possible to get my point across succinctly in just a few words. The lyrics '100 little ways to say I love you' popped into my head and BINGO! There was my idea. Writing this book has been a revelation and an excellent antidote to the verbal diarrhoea I am prone to. I have enlisted the help of some wonderful parents, grandparents and experts to give an extra dimension, as well as covering aspects of parenthood that I have not yet experienced. At the time of writing this my little boy has just turned 4 and started school and so anything beyond this milestone is definitely uncharted territory for me!

Some of these contributors are professional writers, authors and bloggers and if you enjoy reading their work there are links to their sites, just be sure to come back and finish the rest of the book!

The only stipulation I put upon us was that each entry was to be exactly 100 words.

Some of the stories are anecdotal, some poetic, some funny and there are many words of wisdom contained. I have also included some of my favourite quotes on all aspects of parenthood from famous and anonymous sources around the world. I hope you enjoy reading 100 Little Words on Parenthood as much as I did putting it all together.

Birth

'A baby is God's opinion that the world should go on.'
Carl Sandburg

Our Story by Charlie Plunkett
Mum to Cole Jayden born 29th July at home in Brighton weighing 9lbs 5oz to proud parents Charlie and Dave. Charlie is the author of 'The True Diaries' series of books. www.charlieplunkett.co.uk

I experienced such an intense feeling of release, relief and euphoria as you safely slipped from your home of 9 months into the world. The midwife gently lifted you to my chest and as our eyes met, the outside world melted away and in that moment there was only us - you, me and daddy - surrounded by a bubble of the purest love.

Your birth has been beyond a doubt the greatest moment of my life and the gift of motherhood is a treasure I will strive to never take for granted. Welcome to the world our beautiful angel.

'Before you were conceived I wanted you.
Before you were born I loved you. Before
you were here an hour I would give my
life for you. This is the miracle of life.'
Maureen Hawkins

Bonding at Birth by Daisy
Daisy is a cloth-nappy using, breastfeeding and mostly co-sleeping first-time mum (and long-time teacher) - bumbling her way through parenthood and doing what just feels right for her, her husband and their gorgeous little man. www.daisytheclothbummum. wordpress.com

During our anti-natal classes, we were advised to write a birth plan. I was lucky in that our teacher spent a good amount of time advising us what we could do. I'd never thought that I could hold my baby, with the cord still attached to me, until the blood from the placenta had gone back into him. I didn't realise that delayed cord-clamping was so beneficial until I did some research into it. We were lucky that our little man's birth was quite straightforward and allowed us to do this, which also enabled immediate breastfeeding and cuddles.

'The tie which links mother and child is of such pure and immaculate strength as to be never violated.'
Washington Irving

My Birth Beliefs by Charlie Hughes
Mum of 2 beautiful, spirited girls and a freelance writer who also blogs at www.sophiaschoiceuk.blogspot.co.uk and www.madmummymusings.blogspot.co.uk

I believe birth should be a positive experience no matter what your personal circumstances end up being. Trust your body's innate wisdom, trust your instincts and don't fear this most awesome event. Embrace it with strength, confidence and love. Have a plan but be flexible. Each birth you have is unique so this flexibility allows you to change according to the needs of you and your baby. It's an incredible journey to take with your partner and one which will remain etched in the memories of time forever. Remember you have created, nurtured and now birthed the most amazing soul.

'Having a baby is like falling in love again,
both with your husband and your child.'
Tina Brown

A New Baby...and a new me by Jess Sturman-Coombs
Jess is a writer and now very proud mum to two beautiful children. www.jesssturman.wix.com/jess-sturman-coombs

12 pm on a hospital ward, left alone to 'rest' with my new little bundle, a baby boy.

The lights dimmed, everyone sleeping, except for two. I sat in the Family Room drinking strong tea, recalling the lightening events of that momentous day. My son lay in my arms, I think equally stunned but comforted. I held him in front of the window and told him the world was out there, waiting for him and we were here, supporting him. There were a million and one questions awaiting us but together, as a family, we would seek to find some answers.

'Birth is the sudden opening of a window, through
which you look out upon a stupendous prospect.
For what has happened? A miracle. You have
exchanged nothing for the possibility of everything.'
Willie Dixon

Gas and Air by Julia Hughes
In addition to being the proud keeper of two teenagers, Julia has written several action/adventure books. Discover more about Julia and her writing at www.juliahughes. co.uk

My birth plan had 't's crossed, 'i's dotted; I sniggered when people warned that once contractions start, dignity flies out the window. I spent three long painful days in labour. To an audience of nurses, doctors, Tom, Dick and Harry my son made his debut. I still hold a record at Truro hospital: The woman who screamed longest and loudest for someone to get the damn baby out - and how they tried - with forceps then something resembling a sink plunger. Worth it? Within two years I was back on labour ward, armed with my own supply of gas and air!

'My mother had a great deal of trouble with me,
but I think she enjoyed it.'
Mark Twain

Getting to the Land of Hope and Dreams by Ellie Stoneley
Ellie is self-employed, loves local, social media, margaritas, technology for good and does consulting. She became a mother, a first time geriatric mother at 47 to Hope now aged 11 months; beautiful, alert and thriving. She is the writer of 'Mush Brained Ramblings' www.crazypregnantperson.com

I'm old, geriatric in fact, that's what they said. "A miracle IVF worked but ..."

"Pleased you've come this far...", "Older women are at greater risk of miscarriage."

I was good, so good; no rare meat, fizz, caffeine, alcohol, travel, tuna but gallons of water and 2 hours walking every day.

I tripped ... scanned, it was still alive.

Taxi accident ... hospital; scans, ultrasounds fine but no movement.

Terrified 15 days.

It moved again.

I went home. My heart failed. I was unzipped ... it was a girl; fragile, blue.

We both recovered. A fish tank full of Hope wheeled in by a midwife.

> *'It was the tiniest thing I ever decided to*
> *put my whole life into.'*
> *Terri Guillemets*

Instantly Falling Head Over Heels by Louise Hamilton
Proud mummy to Jennifer who at 2 ½ already runs rings around both her parents. She likes to think she spends her days being a domestic goddess but usually she has cake mixture and glitter in her unkempt hair. She is writing a series of books about motherhood. www.mummy-diaries.co.uk

The first time you clap eyes on your new-born baby a rush of instantaneous love and overwhelming emotion courses through your whole body. While you inspect and memorise every inch of new-born skin you question how you ever survived without them, you feel like you've known them your whole life yet every single second is new and memorable. Your new-born baby has its own face, its own expressions, its own personality. It is 50%

mummy and 50% daddy and is a complete miracle. You have never loved anything quite like the way you will love this little bundle of joy.

*'Making the decision to have a child is momentous.
It is to decide forever to have your heart go
walking around outside your body.'*
Elizabeth Stone

Mummy of Two by Tami
Mum to Little Mr A (4 years) and new-born Little Miss A. She blogs about becoming a mum for a second time and family life in general. www.mummyoftwo2.word press.com

For my second baby I wanted a water birth. As soon as I got into the birthing pool I could not believe how calming and relaxing the warm water was. The urge to push came almost immediately and, a bit of gas and air, and 20 minutes later my daughter was born. We were left for a good 20 minutes to enjoy the water and let my daughter "wake up" to the world! I am so glad I got to have a water birth this time. The first thing I said after giving birth was 'Can I do it again!'

*'Birth is not only about making babies. Birth is about
making mothers - strong, competent, capable mothers
who trust themselves and know their inner strength.'*
Barbara Katz Rothman

Having a Baby in a Foreign Country by Charlie Hughes
Mum of 2 beautiful, spirited girls and a freelance writer who also blogs at www.sophiaschoiceuk.blogspot.co.uk and www.madmummymusings.blogspot.co.uk

"Allez, allez, encore, encore!" Those words still ring in my ears. I gave birth to my first daughter in Brittany and wow was it a roller coaster ride. We tried for 3 years before conceiving her and when we did it was in a foreign land, with a different culture and language. I remember clutching my French-English dictionary at every appointment in an attempt to be understood and to understand. A unique experience, daunting, exciting, at times funny. I survived and remember the French nurse weighing my beautiful baby girl as she was yelling and saying "Ohh la la!"

'A new baby is like the beginning of all things-wonder, hope, a dream of possibilities.'
Eda J. Le Shan

Babies

'With moonbeams in hand and stardust in eyes,
you're a baby of heaven drifting down from the sky.'
Debi G

Magical Baby Moments by Charlie Plunkett
Mum to a gorgeous little boy called Cole and author of 'The
True Diaries' series of books. www.charlieplunkett.co.uk

The expression on his face as he drops into a milk-induced sleep.

His hand like a tiny starfish resting in mine.

The strength he has as he grasps his daddy's finger.

The sweet smell of his head and his soft downy hair.

When he waves his arms as though he's conducting an invisible orchestra, performing a Highland fling and riding a motorbike.

How when his daddy holds him, he does a little dance we call the 'Baby Hula'.

The giggles as we play peek-a-boo with him.

How cute he looks rested on his daddy's arm like a baby lion cub.

'What feeling is so nice as a child's hand in yours?
So small, so soft and warm, like a kitten
huddling in the shelter of your clasp.'
Marjorie Holmes

These are a Few of Her Favourite Things by Ellie Stoneley
Ellie is self-employed, loves local, social media, margaritas, technology for good and does consulting. She became a mother, a first time geriatric mother at 47 to Hope now aged 11 months; beautiful, alert and thriving. She is the writer of 'Mush Brained Ramblings' www.crazypregnantperson.com

Tomato
Chorizo
Squid
Spaghetti
Water
Breast feeding
Milky moments
Waking in the morning
Her toys
Little White Ted
Margaret Pollard
Red Rum
Her hands
Clapping
Waving
Kissing
Observing
Chatting
Her feet
Dancing
My singing
Her father's stories
Her precious Granby
The wooden spoon

Nappy changes
Fresh air
Smiling people
Walks
Sunshine
Dolphins
Breeze on her face
The tambourine
Dangling in the waves
Sitting on the beach
Holding sand
Shadows
Pigeons
The baby in the mirror
She loathes Calpol, vests and hats
She adores adventure, craning her head to see what's round every corner but she loves coming home.
My girl.

> *'It is the nature of babies to be in bliss.'*
> *Deepak Chopra*

My Top TIPS For Safer Baby Skincare: by Sharon Trotter RM BSc.
Midwife, mum of five, mother and baby consultant specialising in breastfeeding and baby skincare. Sharon is founder of TIPS Ltd. www.tipslimited.co.uk and www.sharontrotter.org.uk

Anything placed on, in or around your baby has the potential to harm so try to:

- Wash your hands before and after carrying out any baby care.

- Use water only for at least the first month of life, to protect the skin's natural barrier.
- Breastfeeding your baby will help strengthen their immune system from the inside.
- If necessary use a thin layer of barrier cream on the napkin area.
- Once introduced, avoid products that contain sulphates (SLS, SLES), parabens, phthalates, artificial colours and perfumes.
- Rinse baby laundry thoroughly to avoid a build-up of residues that can irritate delicate skin.

*'A baby is a blank cheque made payable
to the human race.'*
Barbara Christine Seifert

Baby Massage Basics by Helen Pritchard
Mum of two, holistic therapist and infant massage instructor who has produced a downloadable DVD 'Massage for Happy Babies' available at www.newstork times.co.uk

Pick a time when the house is quiet and baby and you are calm - it's there somewhere! Using organic grape seed oil warm it in your hands by gently rubbing them together. Hold your warm hands on baby to signal the start of the massage.

Stroke down the arms and chest. Massage the tummy in a clockwise motion following the natural digestive flow. Stroke down the legs and cycle them slowly, then stretch the legs gently. Massage both feet concentrating on the mid-section on the soles of the feet. Wrap baby in a towel and finish with a cuddle.

*'Baby massage is about learning to communicate
your love for your baby through touch. You do
a particular stroke ... and she smiles at you -
and you keep that forever. A great benefit
of baby massage is the bonding.'*
Jill Vyse

Piece for Parents - The Truth by Jo Cammish
New to blogging and new mum to Emilia aged 8 weeks.
wonderments-mjm.blogspot.co.uk

Shock, celebration, nurtured joint creation, epic birth, skin to skin.

Half eaten dinners, cold cups of tea, unopened letters, limited spending.

Dirty clothes on the floor, pots piled high, dust gathering, constant washing machine cycles.

Breastfeeding bonding, cuddles with daddy, startle reflex surprise, tracking with bright eyes.

Exhaustion, anxiety, protective, defensive, fear, arguing and tension, mistakes often made.

Gripping my finger, explosive poo, wriggling body, blowing bubbles, lullabies, splashing in the bath.

Parenting books unopened, conflicting advice, everyone knows best, ear ache on the rise, memory diminishing, shattered.

Cooing, kicking, giggling, smiling, finally some sleep.
Awestruck.
Captivated.
Overwhelmed by Love.

'Take a sprinkling of fairy dust,
An angel's single feather,
Also a dash of love and care,
Then mix them both together.
Add a sentiment or two,
A thoughtful wish or line,
A touch of stardust, a sunshine ray.
It's a recipe, for a Baby Girl truly fine.'
Author Unknown

These Early Days by Helen Braid
Helen lives on the West Coast of Scotland with her husband, boy and baby girl. She works as a graphic designer, makes jewellery and loves to write. You can read more from her blog www.allatseascotland.blogspot.co.uk

The baby has been asserting her authority since her brother started school. It's apparent she doesn't plan on wasting time sleeping... I lowered my cotton romper'd babe, bleary eyed and angry with lack of sleep, to her cot and wished I could climb in too. As I leaned to kiss her cheek she reached out a baby fist and held her mother's face. Gesture enough then, to forgive a day of hair pulling and tears. Sleep has her now, and should until the morning, when my tiny girl will wake afresh and take charge of her mother for another day.

'The story of a mother's life: Trapped between a scream and a hug.' Cathy Guisewite, "Like Mother, Like Daughter"

15

Father's Day by Gemma Crabtree
Mum to Sophie (5) and Tom (3) www.pockettpause.
wordpress.com

It was an unforeseeable time. We were up North visiting
Sophie's grandfather in hospital for Father's Day when
my husband suddenly contracted meningitis.

Two hospitals, two illnesses, one nine-month-old
baby, two extraordinary milestones.

The first happened when I dropped something and
heard the words 'uh-oh'. I looked around then heard
them again: 'uh-oh'. Her first words: so clear, so apt.

The second happened days later, after the funeral.
Eyes, thoughts, focus were elsewhere but she determined
to bring us back. Skipping the crawling she got to her
feet and took her first steps, hauling us, smiling, out of
our grief.

'Children remind us to treasure the smallest of gifts,
even in the most difficult times.'
Allen Klein

Baby's First Christmas by Charlie Plunkett
Mum to a gorgeous little boy called Cole and author of
'The True Diaries' series of books. www.charlieplunkett.
co.uk

It was really important to us that on becoming a family
that we celebrated Christmas together at home, usually
we alternated between our parents. Although our little
boy wouldn't remember this special day we knew we'd
be creating new traditions and memories for years to
come.

We bought a small growing Christmas tree. I made baubles with 'Baby's 1st Christmas' and our names painted on. We dressed Cole in a cute Santa outfit to Skype our parents and took it in turns to cuddle him as we read each other's cards and opened presents. It was the most magical Christmas!

'The best of all gifts around any Christmas tree:
the presence of a happy family all
wrapped up in each other.'
Burton Hillis

Twins

*'It's double the giggles and double the grins, and
double the trouble if you're blessed with twins.'*
Anon

Twin Parent Job Application by Lisa Wildgoose
Single mother of identical twin girls. www.twinstiaras
andtantrums.com

Twin Parent Job Application.

This vacancy is not for the faint hearted, it will be the hardest job you will EVER do!

The perfect applicant will need to be an insomniac and have the arms of an octopus.

You will have a degree in refereeing and be a great mediator. You will have the flexibility of a juggler and the patience of a saint. You do not need to drive because you will be driven, NUTS! The pay is awful and you will have no sick or holiday entitlements... But I promise the emotional rewards will far outweigh all these!

'Two faces to wash, and four dirty hands
Two insistent voices, making demands
Twice as much crying, when things go wrong
The four eyes closing, with slumber song

Twice as many garments, blowing on the line
Two cherubs in the wagon, soaking up sunshine
Work I do for twins, naturally comes double
But four arms to hug me, repay all my trouble.'
Author Unknown

Proof of Telepathic Communication Between Identical Twin Babies? by Anonomum
Writer, blogger and mum of 2 year old identical twins who believes laughter is the key to surviving parenthood. Find out more at www.anonomum.com

Could my 21 month identical twins be telepathic?

Scratchy had a 4 month obsession with jabbing her fingers into Itchy's eyes.

Removing her hands didn't prevent her magnet-like forefinger being drawn to its unfortunate target-looking end. More separation was made and it stopped for a time.

Until one day whilst both sitting in their bouncy chairs, they suddenly looked intensely at each other. I felt I was witnessing telepathic communication. What were they saying? I didn't have to guess for long as Itchy raised her own hand in a trance and then jabbed herself in the eye. Scratchy just laughed.

'There are two things in life for which we
are never truly prepared: twins.'
Josh Billings

Advice for Parents of Twins by Lisa Wildgoose
A single mother of identical twin girls. www.twinstiaras andtantrums.com

Tips for NEW twin parents:

1. If you have no complications YOU CAN have a natural birth!
2. Read anything you can on parenting multiples.
3. Accept all hand me downs with open arms.
4. Freeze big batches of food, so you have ready meals to hand.
5. Don't be afraid to ask for help.
6. Try swaddling; twins are used to being snug.
7. Get them used to cool formula, and then you can feed them anywhere.
8. Keep a kettle just for bottles, so you always have cool water.
9. Have a routine; it will save your sanity!
10. Trust your instincts. You know your babies best!

'Hearts entwined
Twenty fingers, twenty toes
Two sweet babies with cheeks of rose
Born on the same day, two gifts from above
lives entwined, two babies to love.'
Author Unknown

Guidelines for Taking Your Twins to the Park by Anonomum
A writer, blogger and mum of 2 year old identical twins who believes laughter is the key to surviving parenthood.
www.anonomum.com

DO find a park that is enclosed.

DON'T go without a spare pair of hands until they can heel like dogs.

DO encourage one twin's fascination of sitting in the same spot playing with grass if the other wants to climb. Two climbers and one safety net equals disaster.

DON'T have valuables in the pram because you can't watch that too.

DO use the swings to their fullest. They'll love it and they're going nowhere. Relax.

DON'T get into the situation where you're holding both their hands and humping the pram with your groin, you'll look ridiculous.

Written from experience.

> *'With twins, reading aloud was the*
> *only chance I could get to sit down.'*
> *Beverly Cleary*

10 Most Common TWIN Questions... and Answers! By Lisa Wildgoose
Single mother of identical twin girls. www.twinstiaras andtantrums.com

Are they twins? Can't you tell?

Are they identical? Yes, apart from their personalities!

Are they boy/girl? IDENTICAL it's in the name!

Were they produced naturally? None of your bloomin' business!

Buy one get one free? You're hilarious!

I bet you have your hands full? What on earth makes you think that?

How do you cope? I have no choice!

Do twins run in your family? No, 3 years later and I'm still in shock!

Do you know which is which? I bloomin' well hope so, I'm their mother!

Which is your favourite? Depends who is being good that day!

'You can spend too much time wondering which of identical twins is more alike.'
Robert Brault

Questions Questions by Anonomum
Writer, blogger and mum of 2 year old identical twins who believes laughter is the key to surviving parenthood.
www.anonomum.com

With having twins, you're expected to answer extremely personal questions to complete strangers. Write your answers on a billboard and wear around your neck to save time. They'll include:

Are they identical? Reasonable question.

Were they IVF? Unreasonable question.

Do twins run in the family? Non-identical twins do, but identical aren't genetic.

Was it a natural birth? Why?

Will you have any more? Mind your own...

Double Trouble? Not funny after the thousandth time.

I bet you're busy! Well Duh.

I had babies a year apart so I know just what you're going through. Try not to slap this person.

'Not double trouble, but twice blessed.'
Author Unknown

5 Money Saving Tips for Twin Parents by Lisa Wildgoose
A single mother of identical twin girls. www.twinstiaras
andtantrums.com

1. Remember you don't have to buy two of everything, only the essentials like cots and highchairs!
2. Take hand me downs, use car boots, charity shops and second hand sales, everything can be disinfected!
3. Use baby grows for the first six months unless you go somewhere special, this will save time and a lot of stress!
4. Make use of the supermarkets, use their own brands and don't forget to sign up for their baby clubs for freebies and special offers!
5. Double ups - use sleeping bags as foot muffs, use socks as scratch mitts, and a travel cot as a play pen!

'Twice as much to love, two blessings from above.'
Author Unknown

Identical Twins by Lisa Wildgoose.
A single mother of identical twin girls. www.twinstiaras
andtantrums.com

It never ceases to amaze me how different my identical twins are; I presumed that they'd share most traits. Even at a young age the difference is immense. One is slightly cleverer; she won't have to try at anything and will breeze through life with her brains and cuteness. The other isn't stupid by any stretch of the imagination, but she tries harder at everything, she's neat and orderly, and a total perfectionist! I have to remind myself sometimes these two people were supposed to be one? What would that one person have been like? I guess I'll never know...

> *'A good neighbour will babysit.*
> *A great neighbour will babysit twins.'*
> *Anon*

Nappies/Diapers

*'Spread the diaper in the position of the diamond with
you at the bat. Then fold second base down to home
and set the baby on the pitcher's mound. Put first
base and third together, bring up home plate and
pin the three together. Of course, in case of rain,
you gotta call the game and start all over again.'*
Jimmy Piersal

Nappy Dilemmas by Charlie Plunkett
Mum to a gorgeous little boy called Cole and author of
'The True Diaries' series of books. www.charlieplunkett.
co.uk

Towards the end of my pregnancy I purchased a
washable nappy kit. Made from the softest organic
bamboo it was what I would have wanted to put my own
bottom on!

The first few days we used eco disposable nappies
until the meconium passed and then eagerly popped Cole
into his earth friendly nappies and…well they were huge,
I mean really bulky. Hardly any of his clothes fitted over
them and those that did looked comical. The plastic
outer wrappers left red marks on his legs and so we
reverted back to the eco disposables and haven't looked
back since.

'Laughter is like changing a baby's diaper.
It doesn't permanently solve any problems,
but it makes things more acceptable for a while.'
Anon

Cloth Nappies: Easy, Effortless and Cost-Effective by Daisy Daisy is a cloth-nappy using, breastfeeding and mostly co-sleeping first-time mum (and long-time teacher) - bumbling her way through parenthood and doing what just feels right for her, her husband and their gorgeous little man. www.daisytheclothbummum.wordpress.com

When I was pregnant, I stockpiled a load of disposable nappies. But I also looked at cloth nappies (which I'd wanted to use, but felt a little nervous about) and was amazed! Modern cloth nappies are so easy to use, really funky (you can get them with gorgeous, fluffy printed outers) and you don't have to spend hours soaking them. I just put mine in a wet bag and wash at home every 2/3 days. It's simple and has saved us a fortune (under £400 in total) and we have a stash of cute nappies for potential baby no.2!

'Diaper backward spells repaid. Think about it.'
Marshall McLuhan

Your Baby Will Choose to Fill Their Nappy at the Worst Time Possible... by Louise Hamilton
Proud mummy to Jennifer who at 2 ½ already runs rings around both her parents. She likes to think spends her days being a domestic goddess but usually she has cake mixture and glitter in her unkempt hair. She is writing a series of books about motherhood. www.mummy-diaries.co.uk

Jenny did a horrific poo on the plane just as it started moving. The seatbelt sign was on for obvious reasons and Jenny decided to push really hard and let rip with gusto.

She was sitting on my knee; I felt something warm drip down my leg. Even before the plane had gathered enough speed to get us off the runway I had runny poo all over my jeans. The guy sat at the side of me unfortunately had a very sensitive gag reflex and started retching. We caused quite a commotion. On the plus side Jenny found it hilarious.

*'Having someone else to blame when
there is a rude smell in the air.'
Jane Horrocks*

Poo...tatsic! By Charlie Plunkett
Mum to a gorgeous little boy called Cole and author of 'The True Diaries' series of books. www.charlieplunkett. co.uk

I never thought I would be the type of parent that would get excited about the contents of my baby's nappy but I confess I have! When Cole was a week old he did his first proper poo and we told him how proud we were. Since then I've learnt to put a nappy on at lightning speed to avoid being peed on, it is always my first port of call when Cole's upset, a dry nappy makes for a happier baby. We have progressed from yellow poo, to pyramid poos and weaning has introduced a multitude of different colours!

*A baby changes your dinner party conversation
from politics to poops.' Maurice Johnston*

Sleep

*'People who say they sleep like a
baby usually don't have one.'*
Leo J. Burke

Coping with Sleep Deprivation by Charlie Hughes
Mum of 2 beautiful, spirited girls, freelance writer who
also blogs at www.sophiaschoiceuk.blogspot.co.uk and
www.madmummymusings.blogspot.co.uk

When I became a Mum I never realised how much sleep
you lose. I now know why they use sleep deprivation as
torture! Brace yourselves for very little in the early days.
Really do heed the advice to sleep when you can in the
lead up to the birth.

Babies are light sleepers and wake regularly in the
early months. This is normal.

Sleep when baby sleeps and forget about the house. If
like me you find it hard to sleep in the day, at least rest,
lie down, read a magazine, meditate; whatever allows
you to recharge those batteries.

*'Some days I feel like everyone in my world has
plugged themselves into my kidneys. I'm so tired.'*
Gwyneth Paltrow

In Search of Sleep by Daisy
Daisy is a cloth-nappy using, breastfeeding and mostly co-sleeping first-time mum (and long-time teacher) - bumbling her way through parenthood and doing what just feels right for her, her husband and their gorgeous little man. www.daisytheclothbummum.wordpress.com

Sleep. Ah yes, that thing. When the baby fairy picked out our child, she decided to give us a colicky, refluxy mite that really didn't sleep that much. Over the past year what I've discovered is that: Listening to others spout on about their sleeping angels is not a good idea (I zone out and think happy thoughts); colic does go away after about 12 weeks (thank goodness) and that reflux wedges or raising one end of the cot with blocks works miracles. Plus, if your baby is very bad a cranial-sacral massage from an osteopath can be the answer!

> 'The hand that rocks the cradle usually is attached
> to someone who isn't getting enough sleep.'
> John Fiebig

Sleep Deprivation is a Funny Thing by Sofia Harris
Mother of two beautiful boys, Laurence and Jorge-Raphael.

For two weeks after returning to Australia from Europe, my jet-lagged three-month- old son had been waking repeatedly after just half-an-hour's sleep; I was hanging out of my bottom! When my "Milk-Saver" arrived in the post I was eager to get this nifty little device into action, having one breast that would overflow. I slipped the device into my top whilst breastfeeding, smiling as I felt the let-down, knowing that the precious milk was being collected. Moments later I felt a warm wetness and realised I had put the darn thing upside down and the milk was draining onto my belly!

> *'Tired is the new black.'*
> *Amy Poehler*

Groundhog Day by Charlie Plunkett
Mum to a gorgeous little boy called Cole and author of 'The True Diaries' series of books. www.charlieplunkett. co.uk

Upstairs hubby and our favourite TV show await, but you have other ideas and are happily playing peek-a-boo with my nipples. Eventually you drift off into a milk induced sleep with a satisfied smile on your face. I wait a moment taking in your downy hair, angelic face and little fingers still clutching my hand. I wriggle my way across the bed, trying not to wake you. Gently I lower you into your crib and feel my back twinge from nights of performing this manoeuvre. As I tiptoe away I stub my toe, the noise wakes you. We start again...

> *'There was never a child so lovely but his mother*
> *was glad to get him to sleep.'*
> *Ralph Waldo Emerson*

Sleep? What's That? By Victoria Urbanowski-Walls
Victoria is a retail manager and mum to Ethan, aged 8 months.

As a first time mum I scoffed at family and friends who told me 'you sleep when the baby sleeps'. Well I scoff no more. I soon realised that they were right.

I spent the first few weeks of my son's life shuffling around my house like a zombie with a tiny baby perched over my shoulder, and I longed for a nap.

I soon realised that there were a multitude of tasks that I could undertake with my eyes closed, and for this I was thankful.

Having said this the fatigue soon passed, and that's when the fun started.

'A mother's arms are made of tenderness
and children sleep soundly in them.'
Victor Hugo

Sleeping Like a Baby? by Charlotte
A sleep deprived mummy of 'Bob' aged 18 months. You'll find more tales of motherhood, photography and food at www.thecrumbymummy.co.uk

Since Bob came along I have many more hours in the day, 24 in fact! I see most hours, even if only to look at the time and remind myself not to get my hopes up. She may be asleep but only 45 minutes has passed. Celebrations of sleeping through might be a bit premature! I've always been optimistic! I was convinced that when I weaned her she'd sleep. I thought when she could walk she'd tire herself out. I also thought that on the eve of her first birthday the sleep fairy would pay a visit! I was wrong!

'Insomnia: A contagious disease often
transmitted from babies to parents.'
Shannon Fife

Those Early Days as a New Parent: a point of reassurance that you are not alone by HappyMum
A 30-something blogging, part time working and allotmenteering mum of a little cracker. www.mischiefmayhemandmotherhood.blogspot.co.uk

Ten weeks after my son was born amid those blurry days, we went shopping leaving the car in the car park. On our return, I got out the blipper to open the car, but it didn't unlock. I tried several times but the car seemed dead. Great, just what I need. Am I not tired enough! It wasn't until I started to yank the driver's door handle with some frustrated force that I noticed the belongings in the car weren't ours. Three spaces away, my car was locking and unlocking itself, flashing its lights for all to see.

Absolute mortification.

> *'I love sleep. My life has a tendency to fall apart*
> *when I'm awake, you know?'*
> *Ernest Hemingway*

'Who Needs Sleep?' By Mrs W
She can be found blogging at www.milkingitmusings.blogspot.co.uk

The sandman keeps missing me. So weary am I in the small hours, even the snoring I happily put up with. Besides, I wouldn't admit it, but secretly it is actually magical: in my dream-like state I love the cuddles. And yes, even the occasional times when sleep-deprived convenience dictates over all parental policy and little one is in our bed and a foot appears in my eye.

So while we're here at 4.35 am, I'm going to treasure every single moment. If you happen to catch the sandman though, tell him I just want an extra few hours...

'Fatigue is the best pillow.'
Benjamin Franklin

Naptime by 'Older Mum'
A mum for the first time, after years of DJ'ing, gallivanting, working for corporate big wigs, at the not so sprightly age of 39. She has two blogs; one for her personal and creative writing 'Older Mum in a Muddle - the flotsam of a forty something's befuddled mind' www.older-mum.blogspot. co.uk and a supportive resource for mothers over the age of 35, 'Older Mum' www.oldermum.co.uk

Naptime isn't on the menu today.

I need five minutes peace. Clearly, my daughter doesn't.

Thankfully she is content on reading a few books in her cot.

I settle myself on a nearby chair, and open my laptop.

"Mummy - can I talk to you?"

"Sweetheart, it's quiet time."

"Okay, can I play with my teddies?"

"Yes, that's fine."

After five noiseless minutes...

"Mummy, I've got boobies."

I look up to find the legs of monkey and doggy dangling out of her jumper.

"I'm taking boobies out now."

I only wish The Pendulati - my cumbersome breasts - could detach like that!

'A day without a nap is like a cupcake without frosting.'
Terri Guillemets

Rituals by Charlie Plunkett
Mum to a gorgeous little boy called Cole and author of
'The True Diaries' series of books. www.charlieplunkett.
co.uk

We have a nightly bedtime ritual for our 4 year old. First
up he has fun in the bath, then cleans his teeth and has a
relaxing massage with calendula oil before slipping into
soft cotton pyjamas. Snuggled up together on our bed we
read stories and have a little chat about all the fun we
had during the day. We share some kisses and cuddles
before tucking him into his bed. As we leave the room
our favourite thing to do is to take it in turns to call out
'I love you!' whilst blowing kisses and creeping away.

'Always kiss your children goodnight -
even if they're already asleep.'
H. Jackson Brown, Jr.

Breastfeeding

*'A newborn baby has only three demands. They are
warmth in the arms of its mother, food from her
breasts, and security in the knowledge of her presence.
Breastfeeding satisfies all three.'*
Grantly Dick-Read

**Forget Wonder Woman It's (drumroll please) 'Lactating
Girl' by Louise Hamilton.**
Proud mummy to Jennifer who at 2 ½ already runs rings
around both her parents. She likes to think she spends her
days being a domestic goddess but usually she has cake
mixture and glitter in her unkempt hair. She is writing
a series of books about motherhood www.mummy-
diaries.co.uk

There is nothing in this world like the connection,
bond and sense of achievement you will feel when
breastfeeding your baby. As your baby grows, your milk
changes and the relationship between you also evolves;
her eyes become more alert and gaze into your own. As a
mother providing all of the nourishment and nutrients for
your baby you feel a sense of self sustainability! It is not
easy though, there may be hurdles to overcome - thrush,
mastitis or chapped nipples but it is by far the best even
now knowing I gave my baby the best start in life.

'Breastfeeding is a mother's gift to herself,
her baby and the earth.'
Pamela K. Wiggins

My Top TIPS For Successful Breastfeeding: by Sharon Trotter RM BSc.

Midwife, mum of five, mother and baby consultant specialising in breastfeeding and baby skincare and founder of TIPS Ltd www.tipslimited.co.uk and www. sharontrotter.org.uk

- Wear your baby in a sling and stay close, especially in the early weeks.
- Get help with positioning and attachment.
- Always include Dad!
- Supply and demand is the key to successful breastfeeding... this is achieved by baby-led feeding and baby-led weaning.
- Find a local peer support group.
- Breastfeeding is much more than just a way of feeding your baby - it provides the emotional and psychological stability a baby needs to become a confident, relaxed, and independent individual.
- Breastfeeding is a joy - with each feed mothers get a rush of endorphins, which are basically 'happy hormones'.
- Above all, be POSITIVE!

'Breastfeeding is a gift that lasts a lifetime.'
Author Unknown

My Breastfeeding Advice by Daisy
Daisy is a cloth-nappy using, breastfeeding and mostly co-sleeping first-time mum (and long-time teacher) -

bumbling her way through parenthood and doing what just feels right for her, her husband and their very gorgeous little man. www.daisytheclothbummum. wordpress.com

Breastfeeding is, let's be honest, the easiest way to feed your baby. There's no faffing around with bottles, checking the right temperature, remembering to buy milk and... it's very inexpensive! Whilst many people will tell you to avoid nipple shields, really soft ones can be lifesavers and lanolin cream will be your friend whilst your norks toughen up a bit for their new role! Invest in a few good nursing bras, tops that allow you to feed wherever/whenever and some good old nursing pads (did you know that there are washable cloth ones? They're soooo soft and cheap as chips).

'Mother knows breast'
Author Unknown

Breastfeeding Survival Kit by Charlie Plunkett
Mum to a gorgeous little boy called Cole and author of 'The True Diaries' series of books. www.charlieplunkett. co.uk

A seamless bra can help prevent mastitis, as can taking care not to lie on your breasts.

Avoid engorgement by regularly feeding your baby and expressing excess milk. Eat well and always have water to hand. A breast pump, nursing cushions, nipple cream and savoy cabbage are a mum's best friend and asking for help is not a sign of weakness. Breastfeeding support groups are great but sometimes expert advice can be overwhelming and leave you feeling useless. Watching other mums, persevering and allowing yourself to trust that you and your baby know what to do are the keys to success.

> *'My opinion is that anybody offended by*
> *breastfeeding is staring too hard.'*
> David Allen

The End of an Era by Susan Last
Susan is publishing director of Lonely Scribe www. lonelyscribe.co.uk Editor of 'Breastfeeding: stories to inspire and inform' She also blogs at www.thethoughtful publisher.blogspot.co.uk

This morning I got my two-year old out of bed. 'Mik time, Mummy' she piped. I took her back to bed with me and we snuggled up. This morning feed, often her only feed now, is the one time she's quiet and still in the whole long day. My third (and probably last) baby is now a busy toddler and I'm trying to savour every moment of her infancy. Today, when she finished feeding, she looked up at me, put her head on one side, and said decisively 'You are my MUVVER. And I am your DORTER.' And we laughed.

> *'Breastmilk: the gift that keeps on giving.'*
> Author Unknown

Breastfeeding Difficulties

*'While breastfeeding may not seem the right choice for
every parent, it is the best choice for every baby.'*
Amy Spangler

A Little Light on Breastfeeding by Charlie Hughes
Mum of 2 beautiful, spirited girls, freelance writer who
also blogs at www.sophiaschoiceuk.blogspot.co.uk and
www.madmummymusings.blogspot.co.uk

One of the most amazing things you can do for your
baby is to breastfeed; that's a given. However, it doesn't
always come without its trials. After the first two
weeks my nipples were so sore I wasn't sure I wanted to
continue. But if you persevere, it does get easier. Like
any skill it needs lots of practice, patience and trust in
your ability to do it. Link up with a local breastfeeding
support group. They can be a lifesaver when you need
some advice. Above all enjoy this precious, intimate and
special bonding time with your little one.

'Breast milk is better than any udder milk!'
Author Unknown

Mummy Muddling by Charlie Plunkett.
Mum to a gorgeous little boy called Cole and author of 'The
True Diaries' series of books. www.charlieplunkett.co.uk

I thought breastfeeding was the most natural thing in the world. It may well be natural, but it certainly wasn't easy. Two days after Cole's birth and when he latched on I felt a searing pain like razor blades in my nipples. It took several days before tongue-tie was diagnosed, it was easily fixed for Cole but for my poor breasts the damage was already done. I suffered with mastitis and thrush of the nipple coupled with a feeling of total failure when my GP, after observing me feeding Cole, incredulously asked 'Who taught you to do it like that?'

'There are three reasons for breast-feeding:
the milk is always at the right temperature; it comes
in attractive containers; and the cat can't get it.'
Irena Chalmers

Early Days by Sarah Wood
Mum of three and blogger at www.mumofthreeworld. blogspot.com

Trying to get your baby to breastfeed is full-on. And my midwife was tough on me. I had to express every two hours. I gave expressed breast milk and topped up with formula. I found expressing soul-destroying - pumping for an hour to get 20ml out, then an hour off and I'd be pumping again.

Gradually, with the midwife's support, my son started to breastfeed. My husband used to lean over and watch and listen carefully to hear for that first glug when the milk went down. I gave up the expressing and the formula. I hadn't failed! I'd succeeded!

'With his small head pillowed against your breast and your milk warming his insides, your baby knows a special closeness to you,' advised "The Womanly Art of Breastfeeding," originally published by La Leche League in 1958, just two years after the league's first meeting. 'He is gaining a firm foundation in an important area of life - he is learning about love.'

Tongue-tie Troubles by Daisy
Daisy is a cloth-nappy using, breastfeeding and mostly co-sleeping first-time mum (and long-time teacher) - bumbling her way through parenthood and doing what just feels right for her, her husband and their gorgeous little man. www.daisytheclothbummum.word press.com

When our little man was born he had tongue-tie, which wasn't picked up at birth. This made the first few weeks of breastfeeding very difficult and painful as he couldn't latch properly and was getting very hungry and annoyed. Once I'd pushed the midwife into checking properly it was identified and, luckily, we were able to have the tie divided (cut - don't worry, it doesn't hurt them!) Oh my god, what a difference! He was able to suckle properly and we've been happily breastfeeding since. Make sure you get your baby thoroughly checked for this at birth. So important!

'Who fed me from her gentle breast
And hushed me in her arms to rest,
And on my cheek sweet kisses prest?
My Mother.' Anne Taylor

Milky Moments by Ellie Stoneley
Ellie is self-employed, loves local, social media, margaritas, technology for good and does consulting. She became a mother, a first time geriatric mother at 47 to Hope now aged 11 months; beautiful, alert and thriving. She is the writer of 'Mush Brained Ramblings' www.crazypregnantperson.com

We weren't very good at it to begin with, you didn't seem to know how to suck and I kept holding you all wrong. Together we learnt and grew in confidence, your feeding tube was removed and your tongue untied. You fed, you thrived. I felt so very proud.

When you started refusing bottles nobody else could feed you, only me. I was sad for your father and your Granby but secretly, selfishly, indulgently, I loved that it was me nourishing you. Your chubby thighs and wrists were all down to us; you and me.

Breast is best, it's true.

'Mother's milk, time-tested for millions of years,
is the best nutrient for babies because
it is nature's perfect food.'
Robert S. Mendelsohn

Once Bitten, Twice... by Charlotte
A sleep deprived mummy of 'Bob' aged 18 months. You'll find more tales of motherhood, photography and food at www.thecrumbymummy.co.uk

When people asked me if breastfeeding was painful I'd say 'No. Not once I'd reached my second pair of nipples!' My first literally peeled off!

My first attempts we're so painful! It felt like Bob was biting me, even though she didn't have teeth. By the time I left the hospital my nipples were covered in tiny blisters.

Luckily I had a very sympathetic husband, who had first-hand experience of how painful breastfeeding could be. One day, when he was carrying Bob, without his shirt on, she took him by surprise and latched on! He nearly hit the roof!

'There are times when parenthood seems nothing but feeding the mouth that bites you.'
Peter de Vries

You Are Not Alone by Charlie Plunkett
Mum to a gorgeous little boy called Cole and author of 'The True Diaries' series of books. www.charlieplunkett.co.uk

In the days BC (before Cole) I never dreamt there were such things as breastfeeding groups, but then I had never heard of mastitis or cracked nipples before either. On our first visit we were ushered to a screened area, away from the other mums who were happily chatting, drinking tea and appeared to be coping better than me. I learned they were all in fact struggling with one thing or another - too little milk, engorgement, painful latch-on, mastitis, thrush - the list was never- ending. Like survivors on a raft we helped each other through and eventually became breastfeeding experts!

'Nursing does not diminish the beauty of a woman's breasts; it enhances their charm by making them look lived in and happy.'
Robert A. Heinlein

43

Motherhood

*'The moment a child is born, the mother is
also born. She never existed before.
The woman existed, but the mother, never.'*
Bhagwan Shree Rajneesh

(Positive Pregnancy Test) The best is yet to come by
Merryl Polak
Wife, mother, and middle school math teacher. She has
written about her long road to motherhood in her memoir
'Murphy Lives Here'. Merryl has been a guest blogger
and speaker about infertility. You can read her insights on
parenting and more at www.murphyliveshere.weebly.com

My husband and I tried unsuccessfully for almost nine
years to have a baby.

Perhaps that is why I remember taking my pregnancy
test with such clarity. I can still feel my hands shaking
while removing the foil from the test stick. The flashback
causes my heart to beat furiously and a lump to form in
my throat. The hope and anticipation swirling in my
head expanded exponentially when a big YES flashed
across the results window. That moment has been
revisited and celebrated with each smile, sigh, and sound
my daughter has uttered. Motherhood was definitely
worth the wait.

'A mother's joy begins when new life is stirring inside...
when a tiny heartbeat is heard for the very first time,
and a playful kick reminds her that she is never alone.'
Author Unknown

NCT Classes by Claire Hainstock
Mum to Amy, Harry and Joe and company Acting the Party www.actingtheparty.co.uk (friend to Debbie, Louise and Paula - NCT group)

Delight, then fear. OK, keep calm, book classes.

We sit on a stranger's floor with more strangers. The only thing we have in common is the fear in our eyes. We don't take much notice of each other; we get on with breathing and biology. Then one by one, it happens to us, all different, each hitting us like a high speed train. Coffee mornings are organised for us, fear fades.

Eventually we continue meeting by ourselves which we do every week for over ten years. Our friendship steady, so much now in common. All thanks to an NCT class.

'A mother is the truest friend we have, when trials
heavy and sudden, fall upon us; when adversity takes
the place of prosperity; when friends who rejoice with
us in our sunshine desert us; when trouble thickens
around us, still will she cling to us, and endeavour by
her kind precepts and counsels to dissipate the clouds
of darkness, and cause peace to return to our hearts.'
Washington Irving

Pregnant Pause by Helena Wilson-Beevers
Mummy to Lyla and Theo. Freelance writer and blogger. www.stylenest.co.uk/blogs/mummy-mode/

After months of anticipation, the pregnancy test is positive. The bump steadily grows and so does our giddy excitement.

In my 24th week we receive a worrying prognosis. "I'm terribly sorry, but you are in the very early stages of labour." A blur of steroid injections follow. The wait for news feels endless. Then, hope.

Lyla Rose is born at 42 weeks, the most beautiful bundle I could have imagined.

Sleepless delirium and post-birth trauma pales into insignificance. I miss her when she is asleep and she completes me when she is awake. Being a mummy equals heaven on earth.

'A baby has a special way of adding joy in every single day.'
Author Unknown

The Bubble by 'Older Mum'
A mum for the first time, after years of DJ'ing, gallivanting, working for corporate big wigs, at the not so sprightly age of 39. She has two blogs; one for her personal and creative writing 'Older Mum in a Muddle - the flotsam of a forty something's befuddled mind' www.older-mum.blogspot.co.uk and a supportive resource for mothers over the age of 35, 'Older Mum' www.oldermum.co.uk

When did you become a mum?
Was it the thin blue line?
The quickening movements?
The maturing bump?
That first caress of her new born skin?

I became a mum after I had telephone therapy, face-to-face therapy, EMDR therapy...

After breathwork, after homeopathy, after acupuncture...

After I took medication.

And then I finally broke free of the spectral bubble, a treacly membrane that separated me from my daughter, from my body, from my world.

I broke free, beyond my anger, and beyond myself, to life, to feeling, to love, to being.

Post natal illness is a blasphemy to motherhood.

'One word frees us of all the weight and
pain of life. That word is love.'
Sophocles

Not the Maternal Type by Lisa Wildgoose
A single mother of identical twin girls. www.twinstiaras
andtantrums.com

Motherhood didn't come naturally to me! In fact it is a standing joke amongst my family and friends that I was a self-confessed child hater until I hit the age of 32. Not that I would ever do any harm to the screaming, pooing, sticky little beings. I just didn't fancy one ruining MY life! I was the first to admit I was too selfish, I enjoyed doing what I wanted when I wanted; I enjoyed a lie in, I enjoyed my life to the max...

Then I fell pregnant with twins! That God has an amazing sense of humour!

'Even when freshly washed and relieved of all
obvious confections, children tend to be sticky.'
Fran Lebowitz

No One Told Me… by Marsha Taylor-Daniel
A new mum on 1 year's maternity leave.

No one told me…How emotional I would be when I held you.

No one told me…How I would not sleep just to watch you.

No one told me…How often your dad and I would talk of you.

No one told me…How many cute things I would love to buy you.

No one told me…How many chores I would do and still hold you.

No one told me…How many kisses and cuddles I would give you.

No one told me…How easy it would be to love you.

No one told me…What a blessing and gift you would be - lord thank-you!

'Babies are bits of stardust, blown from the hand of God.'
Barretto

Longest Labour in History by Debbie Twomey
Social Networking Conductor, Parental Consultant and a Grand-Mommy Blogger www.djtwomey.com

I always tell people I had the longest labour in history. After 5 years of fostering a little girl who came to me at 18 months, she was finally freed for adoption. My daughter was 6 years old when we finally celebrated the adoption and because she was taking my last name, she referred to it as "getting married". In that spirit, we dressed in our finest frills, went before a judge and were made a true family on September 9, 1999 at 9 am. Armageddon had been predicted this day, but for our family the world had just begun.

'Children are a handful sometimes,
A heartfull all the time...'
Author Unknown

My Baby Had a Liver Transplant by Clare
Mum to two gorgeous boys, Nathaniel (3yrs) and Finn (5yrs). To help other babies like Nathaniel please make sure you and your families are on the organ donation register www.organdonation.nhs.uk

"There's a very rare condition, one in a million chance, it never will be but we have to rule it out," were the words the doctor used. Nathaniel was the one in a million; my perfect little bundle had Biliary Atresia, a rare and life threatening liver condition.

Several operations later he was put on the transplant list. Waiting. Waiting for The Call. Could he hold out until an organ was available? Agonising silence. Nothing on my mind except The Call. Then midnight, my phone rang. A miracle had occurred.

My miracle is now a bubbly, cheeky 3 year old.

'My precious little baby
I have loved you from the start
You are a tiny miracle
Laying closely to my heart
Each day I feel your presence
Each day you heart beats softly

As only I could know
So I'll keep this in a special place
And remember each year through
Of this very special time in my life
The moment I carried you'
Author Unknown

Being a Mum by Charlie Plunkett
Mum to a gorgeous little boy called Cole and author of 'The True Diaries' series of books. www.charlieplunkett. co.uk

I feel like singing from the rafters 'I'm a mum and I love it!' Even on days when sleep eludes me and the washing-up is stacked high in the sink Cole always does something to make me feel blessed to be a mum. If I had known how wonderfully rewarding and awesome being a parent is maybe I wouldn't have left it to the grand age of 38. But on the flip side I've had a career, travelled and been fancy free. Now I'm at a stage in my life where I can truly appreciate the gift that is motherhood.

'A baby will make love stronger, days shorter,
nights longer, bankroll smaller, home happier,
clothes shabbier, the past forgotten,
and the future worth living for.'
Anonymous

A Geriatric Mother (so I'm told) by Ellie Stoneley
Ellie is self-employed, loves local, social media, margaritas, technology for good and does consulting. She became a mother, a first time geriatric mother at 47 to Hope now aged 11 months; beautiful, alert and thriving.

She is the writer of 'Mush Brained Ramblings' www.crazypregnantperson.com

"Are you her Grandmother?" "Are you the nanny?" "No, I'm her mother" "Ohhhhh" ... that's how conversations go! Yes I'm old, Hope, my first and only child was born when I was 47. I'm 48 now and a little weary due to the broken nights and the aching joints that my girl and my great age have given me. I may not have the energy I had when I was 28, but I have love, patience, calm and passion in a way I didn't have then. I love being an older mother I am so blessed. I do dye my hair.

'Thou art thy mother's glass, and she in thee
calls back the lovely April of her prime.'
William Shakespeare

The Older Variety by 'Older Mum'
A mum for the first time, after years of DJ'ing, gallivanting, working for corporate big wigs, at the not so sprightly age of 39. She has two blogs; one for her personal and creative writing 'Older Mum in a Muddle - the flotsam of a forty something's befuddled mind' www.older-mum.blogspot.co.uk and a supportive resource for mothers over the age of 35, 'Older Mum' www.oldermum.co.uk

Can I have another one?
A baby I mean.
I'm 42 in a few days.
My first, and probably last, arrived at 39 years young.
Why did I leave it so late?
Mmmm let me see....

I didn't meet my partner until I was 33.
I still had dreams to fulfil.
I just didn't feel ready...
Psychologically and emotionally ready.
And then I did.
It took two months to fall pregnant.
And now?
Sometimes I wish I had more energy
But, I can impart my daughter with years of experience and emotional insight.
I have no regrets. None at all.

> *'Your children will become what you are;*
> *so be what you want them to be.'*
> *David Bly*

Empowering Things I Have Learned by Alice Grist
Ivy's mum and author of 'Dear Poppyseed A Soulful Momma's Pregnancy Journal' www.alicegrist.co.uk

Since having a baby...

The love comes in waves, gets stronger. It's cosmic.

Stitches and sore bits are nothing. You are mama-warrior!

Follow your instinct. No books or mother-in-laws required.

You are sun and moon to your child. Believe it.

The Mommy Club: kind, understanding and often just as baffled as you.

With a child in your arms you glimpse the kindness of humanity.

With mommy tinted glasses enjoy the purity of your child's soul.

There is no time to worry.
Knowing it won't last forever so live in the moment.
Every day is an adventure. Live like an explorer.

*'You are the bows from which your children,
as living arrows are sent forth.'*
Kahlil Gibran

Since Becoming Parents We've Discovered... by
Monkey's mums Kirsty and Clara
Visit their blog at www.mytwomums.com

We had such strong views before we had Monkey on
how we wanted to parent him, almost all our views have
changed. We said we'd never use a dummy yet at 3 weeks
we did, Monkey hated it! We said we wouldn't co-sleep,
yet it was the only way Monkey would sleep and now at
14 weeks we all love it. What's allowed us to be relaxed
parents is to go with what works and if it doesn't work,
there's always something else we can try. Every moment
with Monkey is precious so we'd hate to waste those
moments worrying.

'It is wisdom to believe the heart.'
George Santayana

Mums Best Friend by Charlie Plunkett
Mum to a gorgeous little boy called Cole and author of
'The True Diaries' series of books. www.charlieplunkett.
co.uk

A mother's best friend is a packet of wet wipes! They
are beyond a doubt the creation of an absolute genius,

a parent no doubt. Before I was a mother I never acknowledged their existence, with the exception of those lemon fragranced wipes my grandma collected from KFC. Now I cannot leave the house without them. They gently wipe my little boy's bottom, clean grubby fingers and remove ketchup from around his mouth. They also, on occasion wipe bird poo from the see-saw. My ode to the humble wet wipe - There is always a place for you in my bag!

> *'Baby wipes are needed because you don't always get to shower.'*
> Pat O'Keefe

A 60's Mum by Mary Dudley
Mum to three 'grown up' daughters and grandma to eight wonderful grandchildren.

A new pram that lifted off to go in the car, wheels that folded all so new and innovative. I had a Baby Burco water boiler, for the lovely terry towel nappies that blew soft on the line. I wore short miniskirts, tights had arrived providing freedom from suspender belts. My baby was able to lie out flat in the pram and sleep contentedly in the garden. I sensed my baby's needs, served fresh food for her. I was not saturated with commercial, useless, so called must haves. I didn't work so I had quality time to enjoy my baby.

> *'Instant availability without continuous presence is probably the best role a mother can play.'*
> Lotte Bailyn

Vulnerability by Joanne Phillips
Author and mother to Lulu aged 4. www.joannephillips.
co.uk

The one thing I was not prepared for on becoming a mum
was how fearful it would make me. No scenario was too
far-fetched, no calamity too implausible. I would lie in
bed convinced that the boiler in the room below my
daughter's would blow up for some reason, and then
horrifying images would follow. I terrified myself with
my thoughts; there was nothing I could do to stop them.
The idea of her growing up safely seemed beyond my
control, and finally I accepted that to some extent it is.
   You do your best. That has to be enough.

> *'Being a mother is learning about strengths
> you didn't know you had, and dealing with
> fears you didn't know existed.'*
> *Linda Wooten*

The World's Greatest Juggler by Tina
Mother of 2 great offspring, Gracie 18 and Thomas
12. Tina is the Editor of Ultimate Wedding Magazine.
www.ultimateweddingmagazine.co.uk

From conception to teenager you worry. You never
stop worrying! Are your children healthy, happy, too
hot, too cold? Do they need more this, more that?
As a working Mum you go into overdrive, do you give
enough attention, affection, time. Am I failing them? Am
I failing myself? We make mistakes, we laugh, the most
important thing is, we do it together, they are my heroes,
I am theirs! We are three musketeers and I have the best

job in the world! The three of us juggle life, school, and work. It sounds dysfunctional. To us it is perfection!

'A worried mother does better research than the FBI' Unknown

Finding the Silver Lining by Lynsey
A proud Mum with two sons. An energetic, fiery red-headed Toddler and a cheeky eight year old who has Cerebral Palsy and wicked sense of humour. www. lynseythemotherduck.blogspot.com

I am grateful when fate decided my child would have severe disabilities, I had the character to cope. As a single mother, at the time, some asked 'Would I give him up?' Those who could think I would give him up because he is not able-bodied are not people I wish to know. I do not look at my son and think he is my disabled son. I look at him and think, he is my eldest son. His disability isn't invisible - far from it. But in the world of my love for him, it doesn't exist at all.

'You've developed the strength of a draft horse while holding onto the delicacy of a daffodil ... you are the mother, advocate and protector of a child with a disability.' Lori Borgman

Being a Single Mother by Lisa Wildgoose
A single mother of identical twin girls. www.twinstiaras andtantrums.com

I'm not going to lie to you; being a single mother is going to be the toughest challenge of all! You have no real support, no back up and you will struggle to make all the difficult decisions alone. There is no one there to pick you up when you fall, and no one to give you a hug and wipe your tears away when you're down...

But console yourself in the knowledge that you will have full use of the remote control, can watch rubbish TV, drink wine and eat chocolate with no one else around to question you!

'After you have a baby, in a few months you work your way up to getting dressed. Then after a few more months, you can start doing your hair, maybe putting make-up on a few times. But you never, ever get back to accessorizing.'
Michelle Pfeiffer

What Motherhood Means by Pippa
Mum to Laila (5yrs) and Cameron (2 ½ yrs)

In no particular order an average day with 2 young children consists of cuddles, kisses, organisation, poo, wee, washing, nose wiping, more kisses and cuddles, a tantrum and a strop, laughter, don't forget your 'please' and 'thank yous', packed lunches, play-dates, pre-school, school, reading, a bit of shouting, more kisses and cuddles, singing badly, crazy dancing, sweets and chocolate, fruit and veg, school run, bath-time, bedtime, a hurt or two, messy rooms, tidying, Barbie and Thomas, trips to the park, naptime, more laughter, some television, tears, more magic cuddles and kisses, a few 'I wants' and many 'I love yous'.

'Any mother could perform the jobs of several air traffic controllers with ease.'
Lisa Alther

Firsts by Charlie Plunkett
Mum to a gorgeous little boy called Cole and author of
'The True Diaries' series of books. www.charlieplunkett.
co.uk

I will never forget the moment we first set eyes on each
other, your first smile, your first cry, the first time you
rolled over, learning to crawl and those first teeth coming
through. Your first word was 'mama' loud and clear and
the expression on your face at your first taste of
food was precious. Your very first steps are my fondest
memories beside a tree where your daddy and I were
married. First days at nursery and school made me so
proud to be your mummy and who can tell what other
firsts there are still to come.

*'When you have brought up kids, there are
memories you store directly in your tear ducts.'*
Robert Brault

The Many Occupations of a Mother by Victoria
Urbanowski-Walls
Victoria is a retail manager and mum to Ethan, aged
8 months.

Before I was married I never wanted children, I was more
than happy to play "favourite aunty" to my nieces and
nephews. I never imagined myself cleaning up toys,
doing endless amounts of laundry or sterilising bottles
day and night, but here I am. I've gone from a retail
manager to a chef, cleaner, personal shopper, security
guard, chauffeur and nurse, and I wouldn't have it any
other way. Being a first time mum is the most terrifying

job I've ever had, but also the most rewarding and I wouldn't change it for the world.

I love my new job!

> *'Being a full time mother is one of the highest salaried jobs... since the payment is pure love.'*
> Mildred B. Vermont

Coming to Terms with Disability by Karen Marquick
Mum of Samuel aged 9 years, Oliver aged 2 ½ years and Isabella, aged 18 months. www.womanwifeandmum. blogspot.co.uk

When I gave birth to my perfect 6lb 8oz bundle of joy no-one could have predicted the rocky road ahead and the challenges I would face as a mother, or that he faces forever. My eldest son was born with a disability that was undiagnosed for nearly 5 years. He has chromosome 22q11 deletion syndrome. He was diagnosed following developmental and speech delay, and he has learning difficulties. I have felt a mixture of emotions over the years, and shed many tears both of joy and sadness.

My amazing son is now 9 and it still overwhelms me at times.

> *'The child must know that he is a miracle, that since the beginning of the world there hasn't been, and until the end of the world there will not be, another child like him.'*
> Pablo Casals

How Motherhood Changes You by Susanne Remic
A mother of three, trained primary school teacher and freelance writer. She handles social media at

www.babyhuddle.com and blogs at www.ghostwriter mummy.co.uk She is co-creator of Maternity Matters, a site dedicated towards raising awareness of birth trauma.

When I became a mum, I inherited super powers. I now have the ability to hear the cry of my child amongst a sea of others. I now have the ability to feel their pain, fear, joy and happiness. I now have the ability to see right through to their dreams, hopes and desires. I now have the ability to climb mountains, fight monsters and cross oceans to be the mum they need me to be. I now know the true meaning of true and utter love, pain and hope. Those are my super powers - my gift from my children.

> *'Mother love is the fuel that enables a normal human being to do the impossible.'*
> *Marion C. Garretty*

My Tom by J.M. Worgan
Mother to two young boys. Her youngest son has Autistic Spectrum Disorder. Author of 'Life on the Spectrum. The Preschool Years. Getting the Help and Support You Need' www.goodreads.com/JMWorgan

My Tom is four and has Autistic Spectrum Disorder. There are many comments when people meet him, including 'he doesn't look autistic, how awful for you' and 'I am so sorry'. Although people do not mean to inflict hurt with their words they do. So here is the truth. Autism is a 'hidden' developmental disability, which affects the person socially, behaviourally and communicatively.

Above all though, he is my little boy. He does not 'look autistic', I do not think life is so 'awful' and I am not sorry that I have him in my life. He makes life special.

'Doctors look at me and say I'm autistic, but my mummy holds me and says I'm perfect.'
Anon

Would I Do It Again? by Mary Dudley
Mum to three 'grown-up' daughters and grandma to eight wonderful grandchildren.

Teething baby, terrible twos, the first day at school, they will not eat.
'I want to!'
'Can I have?'
'Because everyone else has!'
Challenging your opinions, finding their own personality.
They will not wash, will not tidy their room.
Cannot get them out of the bathroom.
The first boyfriend.
You are awake because they are out.
They live together.
The last boyfriend who becomes your son-in-law.
Finally in their forties you look at them with huge relief.
They are just fine.
My family have tripled with son-in-laws and grandchildren.
Would I do it all again?
YES OF COURSE I WOULD!

*'A mother's happiness is like a beacon, lighting
up the future but reflected also on the past in
the guise of fond memories.'*
Honoré de Balzac

My Handbag by Charlie Plunkett
Mum to a gorgeous little boy called Cole and author of
'The True Diaries' series of books. www.charlieplunkett.
co.uk

Before I became a mum my handbag was small and
rarely full; my mobile, purse, a bottle of water and
I was good to go. Nowadays my bag would make
Mary Poppins envious. It is a veritable filing cabinet of
necessities including the above but also wipes, tissues,
spare pants, a change of clothes, snacks, arnica tablets
and cream, BFP free water containers, more snacks, a
purse full of membership cards to child friendly places,
sun lotion, sunglasses and bubbles. If I squish everything
I can also fit our raincoats and a couple of small toys
to entertain.

*'My purse is always filled with stuff I didn't put there,
from leftover Tootsie Rolls to wet wipes that got
squished to the bottom. It makes me laugh every day.'*
Nia Vardalos

Mummy Knows Best by Susan Spence
Mum of 4, wife of 1. Her lovely biggest boy has Asperger
Syndrome. www.mumof4wifeof1.blogspot.co.uk

If there's one thing my four children have taught me, it is
that Mummy knows best.

The toddler that arranged stacking cups into order over and over again? The 2 year old that couldn't eat his meals unless it was with the same spoon? The 6 year old that knew and could identify every make and model of car in existence? A diagnosis of Asperger Syndrome was the result of a long and difficult battle but was not a shock, and has made me more certain that parents know their children better than anyone else can. Mummy always knows best.

'The more people have studied different methods of bringing up children the more they have come to the conclusion that what good mothers and fathers instinctively feel like doing for their babies is the best after all.'
Dr. Benjamin Spock

Making Memories by Victoria Pearson
Victoria lives behind a keyboard, surrounded by the chaos being married with three children, a dog and a very clumsy cat creates. When she isn't running around screaming, "Be careful" or picking up after someone she is generally to be found writing stories. www.victoria-pearson.webs.com

When I was pregnant with my first son, I started making him a cot quilt. I am a terrible seamstress, so he got it for his first birthday, but I was very proud of it, and he used it for a long while. My daughter used it too, and gave it to my youngest on his first birthday. He got very attached to it, still sleeps with it now (he is five). He calls it his Noo-Noo (because as a toddler he had it at 'night-night time' and he couldn't say that). Perhaps one day my grandkids will use it.

*'A mother should be like a quilt, keep the children
warm but don't smother them.'*
Author Unknown

Becoming a Mother by Suzanne Whitton
Mum to three gorgeous children and 1 crazy pooch. You
can find her blogging about parenting at www.3children
andit.blogspot.co.uk

I was not at all prepared for Motherhood. I found the
transition from being one half of a married couple to
becoming a responsible Mother overwhelming. As
someone who does not react well to change, for those
first few days I felt a strange mix of love and resentment
for this new person who I was now utterly responsible for
and hugely under-equipped to deal with. There were times
when I would hanker longingly after my old, carefree life
but I soon became accustomed to this new world - one
where my own needs and wants would take second place.

*'A mother is a person who seeing there are only
four pieces of pie for five people, promptly
announces she never did care for pie.'*
Tenneva Jordan

Things My Mother Used to Say to Me by Charlie Plunkett
Mum to a gorgeous little boy called Cole and author of
'The True Diaries' series of books. www.charlieplunkett.
co.uk

Don't run with that you will have your eye out! Eat your
crusts if you want your hair to be curly, don't step on the
cracks in the pavement, the bears will get you, don't cry,

you will look like a horse, never squeeze a spot by your mouth. It's unlucky to put an umbrella up indoors, new shoes on the table, or walk under a ladder, always blow a kiss to a magpie. Respect your elders; be kind to your sisters. My favourite of all and one I say to my little boy is, 'Let mummy kiss it better.'

> *'Who ran to help me when I fell,*
> *And would some pretty story tell,*
> *Or kiss the place to make it well?*
> *My mother.'*
> *Ann Taylor*

Advice for Mums

*'The best advice from my mother was a
reminder to tell my children every day:
Remember you are loved.'*
Evelyn McCormick

A Note to My Newly Mummy Self! by Karen Cannon
Mum to Lexie aged 2yrs. She blogs at
www.365pearlsofwisdom.blogspot.com

Dear Karen,

Now baby is here you can see that parenthood is
nothing like you expected! But don't fret, these wise
words will steer you on the right path. When everybody
says "sleep when baby sleeps" they are right, do it!
Colic is stressful and heart-breaking but is doesn't last
forever. Don't wear anything white until baby is at least
18 years old!

Breastfeeding in public is yours and baby's right; be
confident and believe in what you're doing. Don't worry,
baby will sleep throughout the night, eventually! You
will be confident in what baby needs to feel contented.

Good Luck!

'Trust yourself. You know more than you think you do.'
Benjamin Spock

Post Natal Depression (PND) by Charlie Hughes.
Mum of 2 beautiful, spirited girls, freelance writer who
also blogs at www.sophiaschoiceuk.blogspot.co.uk and
www.madmummymusings.blogspot.co.uk

It's never expected. It's the hardest thing to accept that
we just don't feel ourselves having given birth to this
amazing being. We're not feeing instant love, we feel
detached, uneasy, scared. PND is more common than we
realise. It's only in recent years with more celebrities
opening up about their experiences that the stigma
attached to this often crippling illness is lessening.
Having suffered myself, it's important to know that you
do get better. The feelings eventually pass, you'll finally
bond with your baby and they won't love you any less.
But above all talk to someone and get help.

'A woman is like a teabag. Only when in hot
water do you realize how strong she is.'
Nancy Reagan

Take Time by Meghan Peterson Fenn
Author of Bringing up Brits and mum to three lovely
children. www.bringingupbrits.co.uk

Life as a busy mother of three is hectic and demanding -
all those jobs to get done for work, house and kids. The
never-ending 'to do' list and various schedules dominate
our lives. So let's STOP. Stand still. EMBRACE. Let's
spend time together NOT getting things done. Let's
just BE together as a family and celebrate everything
GOOD we have and the LOVE we feel for each other.
I remember something my own mother told me the

day I gave birth to my first baby. "The dishes can wait" she said. How absolutely right she was. The dishes can wait.

'If I had my child to raise all over again, I'd build self-esteem first, and the house later. I'd finger-paint more, and point the finger less. I would do less correcting and more connecting. I'd take my eyes off my watch, and watch with my eyes. I'd take more hikes and fly more kites. I'd stop playing serious, and seriously play. I would run through more fields and gaze at more stars. I'd do more hugging and less tugging.' Diane Loomans, from "If I Had My Child To Raise Over Again"

Enjoying Life as a Single Mother by Lisa Wildgoose
A single mother of identical twin girls. www.twinstiaras andtantrums.com

Being a single mother doesn't mean your life has to stop... It just means your life has to change! Instead of sitting in on a Saturday night and feeling fed up. Treat yourself to a bottle of wine and a takeaway!

The great thing about being a single mum is when the kids go off to their dad, grandparents, friends you get the chance to have some proper me time.

Use it wisely! Do not spend it cleaning the house, doing the ironing or making dinner.

Make the most of it, put your feet up; you have earned that rest... Enjoy it!

*'You know your life has changed when going to the grocery store by yourself is a vacation.'
Unknown.*

Cool, Calm Parent by Hollie Smith
Mum, blogger, journalist and author of parenting books
(but sadly no expert). www.holliesmith.co.uk

I was probably setting myself up as a hypocrite when I wrote a book called 'Cool, Calm Parent'. I am so not a cool, calm parent myself. It offers to help parents stop getting angry with their kids so much. But the truth is, a bit of shouting now and then is useful. If your kids leave home and enter a world where shouty people come as a surprise, then you'll have done them a disservice! I do think 'let the little things go' is good advice, though. And sometimes you should let the medium-sized and big things go, too.

'Some mothers are kissing mothers and some are
scolding mothers, but it is love just the same,
and most mothers kiss and scold together.'
Pearl S. Buck

Pushchair Etiquette: The Rules of the Road/Pavement
by Charlie Plunkett
Mum to a gorgeous little boy called Cole and author of
'The True Diaries' series of books. www.charlieplunkett.
co.uk

Once you get behind the wheels of a pushchair you'll need to know the rules. Who to give way to and when it's OK to overtake. The order of priority I think should be as follows -

Part One - Give way to any parent pushing a buggy containing a new-born. They take preference because they're most likely sleep deprived and not fully aware of anything outside of the wonderful bubble of being with a new baby. They will also still be coming to grips with 'driving' their pushchair and should be forgiven if they accidently run over your toes.

> *'The one thing children wear out faster*
> *than shoes is parents.'*
> *John J. Plomp*

Pushchair Etiquette: Parts Two, Three and Four by Charlie Plunkett
Mum to a gorgeous little boy called Cole and author of 'The True Diaries' series of books. www.charlieplunkett.co.uk

Part Two - Parents with a determined look in their eyes, power walking/sprinting with a child in their buggy are likely to be running late for nursery. Safest to let them overtake as the speed they'll have built up would make stopping impossible.

Part Three - Take into account the terrain. If you are on a hill allow the person travelling downwards to go first, after all momentum is on their side.

Part Four - Anyone who has managed to attach a week's groceries to their handlebars deserves respect and the entire width of the pavement to avoid unnecessary spillage.

> *'Don't base your parenting skills on your ability to*
> *keep a hat on your child'*
> *Jerry Seinfeld*

Pushchair Etiquette: Parts Five, Six and Seven by Charlie Plunkett
Mum to a gorgeous little boy called Cole and author of 'The True Diaries' series of books. www.charlieplunkett.co.uk

Part Five - If you find yourself playing chicken with a double buggy, or one of those gigantic Victorian style prams, always let them pass first otherwise they will simply mow you and your ergonomic buggy down.

Part Six - Whenever faced with the dilemma of squeezing past another buggy always offer your biggest smile, a real upturned smiley mouth not just baring your teeth. This can look as though you are growling and could be construed as 'buggy rage'.

Part Seven - Finally, always be aware of those behind you, stopping suddenly could cause a pile up.

Happy driving!

'Sweater, n.: garment worn by child when its mother is feeling chilly.'
Ambrose Bierce

Fatherhood

*'Fatherhood is pretending the present
you love most is soap-on-a-rope.'*
Bill Cosby

Becoming a Father by Richard Denman
Dad of two now grown up young people who are also like best friends. He tries hard not to stumble over himself, which is quite a task. Richard is author of the poetry book 'Love Life' (available from Amazon).

'What? Now! 6 am! And so the sleep deprivation begins.' My response to Katie telling me she was in labour a certain Sunday morning in January 1992. A most wonderful day. 'Right! Maternity hospital might be a good place for you then.'

Delivery time! They have concerns for my wife as our baby is in the breech position and, despite encouragement, has decided to enter the world this way. A sit in even before birth! It was a difficult delivery with anxiety all around. Then out popped the legs; 'Katie. I can definitely tell you that our baby's a girl!'

*'Yes, having a child is surely the most beautifully
irrational act that two people in love can commit.'*
Bill Cosby

Birth by Lewis
Blogger and first time dad to a seven month old called
Cam. www.newbabber.blogspot.co.uk

I always thought I'd stay at the head end. My wife's head
that is. The baby's head was at the end I hadn't thought
I'd be. But I was. That was the thing with labour. It
changed everything. Simultaneously magical and a little
like something from a horror movie; it was a life defining
moment for me. Squeamishness banished to the back of
my mind, feeling utterly helpless but wanting nothing
more than to help. Excitement, hope and trepidation in
equal measure. Then there was a baby. Oh my God,
there's my baby. Tears of unimaginable joy fell from me.

'When a child is born, a father is born...
he has seen the creation of the world.'
Frederick Buechner

Parents at Last by Dave Plunkett
Proud dad to a wonderful son called Cole and husband
to Charlie.

9 months +1 week of waiting and the moment is finally
upon us. My wife is about to give birth, and we cannot
believe we are about to be parents!

As I cut the umbilical cord the emotion really hit me.
To see our son Cole open his eyes was a great feeling.
I was so proud of my wife and to think she did it all
without any drugs. It was then that I realised what a
miracle childbirth is. I found myself sitting watching
my son sleep all through that evening, as I was still in
disbelief.

'Until you have a son of your own... you will never know the joy, the love beyond feeling that resonates in the heart of a father as he looks upon his son. You will never know the sense of honor that makes a man want to be more than he is and to pass something good and hopeful into the hands of his son.'
Kent Nerburn

Meeting for the First Time and Ever After by Sam Coleman
Writer, blogger and stumbling father to a little girl way ahead of her time and often ahead of him. He is as lost in the world as you are. You'll find him muttering at www.dustandlove.wordpress.com

You fall in love. Your heart beats so hard you think your ribs are going to split. When you hold them the world melts into oblivion. They bring you to your knees when they cry. You run to the ends of the earth just to be with them. It's a precious thing to have someone love you this much. And they do love you. You feel it in their chest when you sooth them to sleep. You hear it in their voice when they sing. You smell it on their skin. It's terrifying and joyous. It's yours for the taking.

'Small child-once you were a hope, a dream. Now you are reality. Changing all that is to come. So small. A flick of star stuff. A mind to touch the edges of the universe. A love to hold our hearts forever.'
Charlotte Gray

In the Beginning by Mark Richards
Mark started writing a weekly column about his children ten years ago. He's gone from nativity plays and party

bags to teenage angst, slamming doors and boyfriends he's - wisely - not told about. You can find his 'Best Dad I Can Be' books on the Kindle and follow the battle with his teenage children on his website www.best dadicanbe.com

The moment I first held my son. He's at university now - doing a joint degree in Engineering and Sarcasm. But 19 years on, writing this still brought tears to my eyes.

"Would Daddy like to hold him?"

The midwife passed me my son. My son. My first child. Brown eyes. Just like me.

Cricket, football, walks on the beach... What we wouldn't do together.

"Are you alright with him, Dad?"

"What? Yes. Yes. He's just perfect."

My son gazed up. Looked at his Daddy for the first time. Then he emptied his little bladder all over my lucky green shirt.

'The greatest gift I ever had came from God;
I call him Dad!' Author Unknown

Becoming a Father Again by Richard Denman
Dad of two now grown up young people who are also like best friends. He tries hard not to stumble over himself, which is quite a task. Richard is author of the poetry book 'Love Life'(available from Amazon).

'Rich. I'm in pain. I was in the bath and ....'

'Your waters have broken in the bath?!'

Just then a second labour pain started. 'I'm calling the midwife,' I said.

Our second baby was a home delivery. Labour was in full swing as the midwife arrived. We lived down a pedestrian lane so myself and a friend rushed to get the gas and air to the house for a desperate Katie who started gulping as our baby boy wasn't hanging about. The labour was just two hours! 'Phew!'

The midwife turned and offered me gas and air; 'Yes please!!'

'A father carries pictures where his money used to be.'
Author Unknown

2.30 am by Ben Wakeling
Award-winning dad blogger and the author of 'Goodbye Pert Breasts' www.goodbyepertbreasts.com

Before I became a dad I barely even knew that 2.30 am existed. It's a strange time, but one I have become all too familiar with now I have a baby. It's a time of lamp-lit streets, roaming cats, a house silent save for the snuffles of your newborn as you rock her to sleep in a darkened room, illuminated by the light of awful television. Why would they broadcast any decent programmes? No-one is meant to be awake at 2.30 am. You miss your bed, naturally; but there's something magical about being with your daughter, shrouded in darkness, having a cuddle.

'There's something like a line of gold thread
running through a man's words when he talks to
his daughter, and gradually over the years it gets to
be long enough for you to pick up in your hands
and weave into a cloth that feels like love itself.'
John Gregory Brown

My Favourite Current Routine Is "The Trap" by Ben Hatch
Father and author of Radio 2 Book of the Year 'Are
We Nearly There Yet? 8000 Misguided Miles Round
Britain in a Vauxhall Astra'. Ben has also written three
guidebooks for Frommer's with his wife Dinah. The
guidebooks are a mixture of helpful and humorous
tips on holidaying with children, quirky reviews of
attractions, and incendiary arguments with his wife
about, among other things, short-clawed otters. (Books
available from Amazon).

For 3 years it's been my son's goodnight. The Trap starts
when my son (5) wraps his legs round my midriff. He
says: "You're trapped!" His arms encircle my neck.
    Noosed, I stand as he clings on. "The shark's got me,"
I cry. He laughs evilly and usually says, "Actually I'm
a crocodile/dinosaur/nasty dog." "I meant a crocodile/
dinosaur/nasty dog's got me," I say. He touches the
ceiling. I throw him on the bed. I say: "That was a good
one. Goodnight." The longer it continues the more it
evolves and the surer I am he will always remember:
"The Trap".

'A boy is a magical creature you can lock him out of
your workshop, but you can't lock him out of your
heart. You can get him out of your study, but you can't
get him out of your mind. Might as well give up he is
your captor, your jailer, your boss and your master a
freckled-faced, pint-sized, cat-chasing bundle of noise.
But when you come home at night with only the
shattered pieces of your hopes and dreams, he can
mend them like new with two magic words Hi, Dad!'
Alan Marshall Beck

Pride by James Smith
Father of three wonderful boys. When he finds a spare moment he attempts to write fiction. He is a founding member of a short story group who publish seasonal collections to raise money for charity. www.shortstories group.blogspot.co.uk and blogs at www.jamessm1th. wordpress.com

I spent too many hours sitting in stony silence returning from my son's football matches - suppressing my anger at his silly behaviour during the morning.

I spent too many hours being chastised by my wife for being too hard on my son.

I now spend many hours looking at the trophies and personal awards my son has - Player of the Season, County Cup Winners medals - but even these physical objects cannot eclipse the sense of pride when his coach stops me and tells me how good my son is getting. Perhaps I was a little hard on him, or not.

'No man stands so tall as when he stoops to help a child.'
Abraham Lincoln

Advice for New Fathers

'It is much easier to become a father than to be one.'
Kent Nerburn, Letters to My Son: Reflections on
Becoming a Man, 1994

The Role Reversal by Sam Coleman
A writer, blogger and stumbling father to a little girl way
ahead of her time and often ahead of him. He is as lost
in the world as you are. You'll find him muttering at
www.dustandlove.wordpress.com

Remember this. It's not all about you anymore. But don't
ever forget that she loves you. She's just listening for
the pain filled squeal from the next room. She's worrying
about how to keep a tiny human being alive and
entertained. She's worrying that her breast milk just isn't
enough. She's worrying that her skills as a Mother just
aren't up to the task. She's worrying. She's focusing all
her love on the children like laser guided missiles. Even if
you aren't swimming in oceans of passion you're still
swimming in the same sea. Please don't forget you love her.

'Once you become the mommy or daddy in your child's
world, it is the only world in which you exist, no matter how
much you fancy there is a separate world of your own.'
Robert Brault

Dad Skills by Benjamin Tipping
Blogger, runner and dad to two children, Matilda and
Henry. www.mutteringsofafool.com

Dad skills…

As a new dad it is vitally important to learn new skills
and the most important of all is how to sniff a nappy.
Other dads will look on in awe as you raise your baby up
into the air, put its bum against your nose and inhale
deeply. You then pronounce loudly 'WET' 'DRY'
'WIND' 'POO' with absolute certainty. No need to peel
back the layers and peer in the nappy for you. Done and
dusted in one sniff. Learn this skill and you are now a
level 2 dad and en route to becoming a legend.

*'I think I am (good at changing diapers). I could
have a race-off with some other dads out there.*
Matthew McConaughey

Belief by Lewis
Blogger and first time dad to a seven month old called
Cam. www.newbabber.blogspot.co.uk

As if a baby itself wasn't exciting enough, each one
comes with a free gift: doubt.

Doubt in your own ability as a parent. Doubt in
everything you do. Are we changing him often enough?
Is he feeding well? Is he too hot? Too cold? Should he be
sleeping more/less/at all? Everyone else seems to be an
expert; conflicting advice comes at you from all directions.
Well, let me add to that with my own: believe.

Believe in yourself and your instincts. Believe that you
know your baby better than anyone else does. Believe
and you will be just fine.

'The guys who fear becoming fathers don't understand that fathering is not something perfect men do, but something that perfects the man. The end product of child raising is not the child but the parent.'
Frank Pittman, Man Enough.

Teething

'*Adam and Eve had many advantages, but the principal one was that they escaped teething.*'
Mark Twain

Teething Pains by Charlie Plunkett
Mum to a gorgeous little boy called Cole and author of 'The True Diaries' series of books. www.charlieplunkett. co.uk

I have so much sympathy for a teething baby. Imagine the worst toothache, then combine that with a lack of being able to communicate and you are somewhere in the vicinity of how they must feel. During the day they can mostly be pain-free but night time can be another matter! I discovered babies are more easily distracted during the day. At night, when they are lying down, excess saliva goes into the ear canal causing ear and toothache. Thankfully it is just a phase and once those little fangs have burst through you will have your happy baby back.

'*When you are a mother, you are never really alone in your thoughts. A mother always has to think twice, once for herself and once for her child.*'
Sophia Loren

Teething Problems by Lisa Wildgoose
A single mother of identical twin girls. www.twinstiaras
andtantrums.com

Teething = 2 years of hell for most parents! It's like your child having a persistent illness that just won't go away. You will spend many a sleepless night worrying what to do for the best... When in reality you can't do much at all!

But I had a secret weapon... Teething powders! They're made from all sorts of herbal ingredients but they always managed to calm my little ones. They saved my sanity. I didn't know what was mixed in these miracle packets, and quite frankly I didn't care!

They were definitely the best teething product I ever bought!

'Motherhood has a very humanizing effect.
Everything gets reduced to essentials.'
Meryl Streep

The T Word by Louise Hamilton
A proud mummy to Jennifer who at 2 ½ already runs rings around both her parents. She likes to think she spends her days being a domestic goddess but usually she has cake mixture and glitter in her unkempt hair. She is writing a series of books about motherhood. www.mummy-diaries.co.uk

Teething: when it happens you are in a whole world of pain. Say the word 'teething' to someone who doesn't have children and they will pull a sympathetic face and say "aww are they having an off day?" AN 'OFF' DAY?

Are you serious? At night I am up every hour, I haven't seen a smile in days, poor baby whimpers and then sudden outbursts of murderous screaming, she has a fever, constant stream of snot and dribble, red cheeks, more diarrhoea nappies than I care to count and is trying to eat my fingers - failing that the whole cot!

'Parents are the bones on which children cut their teeth.'
Peter Ustinov

Teething? By Gemma Crabtree
Mum to Sophie (5) and Thomas (3). She writes about life with two littlies down under at www.pockettpause. wordpress.com

Teething?
It must be teething.
It must.
It definitely is.
But she's only 6 weeks old.
But we've done everything else, everything.
Maybe she's hungry.
But you've just fed her.
Then it's probably wind.
(pat, pat, pat, pat)
Nothing.
Have you checked her nappy?
(lifts her in the air and sniffs)
Clean.
What's she doing now?
I'm not sure.
Look, her fist's in her mouth again.
Is she dribbling?

Her cheeks look a bit red.
Get the book.
There: look, teething, symptoms...
You're right. I bet we'll see that first tooth tomorrow.
I bet.
Or maybe she's just hungry?
(sigh)

> *'How beautifully everything is arranged by*
> *Nature; as soon as a child enters the world,*
> *it finds a mother ready to take care of it.'*
> *Jules Michelet*

Teething Tips by Charlie Plunkett
Mum to a gorgeous little boy called Cole and author of
'The True Diaries' series of books. www.charlieplunkett.
co.uk

Tips that helped us through those tricky teething
months included taking Cole to see a cranial osteopath.
Osteopathy can help with feeding, colic, sleeping and
teething. Giving him cucumber and frozen banana
helped to cool his gums, we raised his head slightly
when he was sleeping by placing a towel under his
mattress and used the homeopathic remedy, chamomilla,
when he appeared to be in discomfort. His favourite
teething toy was the famous 'Sophie the giraffe' made
from 100% natural rubber and we were big fans of
cool dribble bibs with a double layer to absorb all that
teething dribble.

> *'People often ask me, "What's the difference between*
> *couplehood and babyhood?" In a word? Moisture.*

Everything in my life is now more moist. Between your spittle, your diapers, your spit-up and drool, you got your baby food, your wipes, your formula, your leaky bottles, sweaty baby backs, and numerous other untraceable sources…all creating an ever-present moistness in my life, which heretofore was mainly dry.'
Paul Reiser

Weaning and Picky Eaters

*'In general my children refuse to eat anything
that hasn't danced on television.'*
Erma Bombeck

Miss Independence by Merryl Polak
Wife, mother, and middle school math teacher. She has
written about her long road to motherhood in her
memoir 'Murphy Lives Here'. Merryl has been a guest
blogger and speaker about infertility. You can read
Merryl's insights on parenting and more at www.
murphyliveshere.weebly.com

My daughter used to pull my shirt down when she was
hungry. Her take charge behaviour started at about
four months and continued until her seventh month.
In her eighth month of life, she stopped. I would offer
her nutrition, and she would look interested. Her interest
was fleeting because each time she would bite and release
her latch. Stunned at every feeding, I would wonder
what happened as she crawled away to focus on other
adventures. My paediatrician explained that she had
weaned herself. He congratulated me for cultivating
the first moment of my child's independence. Success
sometimes hurts.

'It is one thing to show your child the way,
and a harder thing to then stand out of it.'
Robert Brault

Tips for Weaning by Lisa Wildgoose
A single mother of identical twin girls. www.twinstiaras
andtantrums.com

Babies spit out baby rice, not because they don't like the taste, it's the texture their not keen on. They've only been used to liquid!

Mix their first tastes with baby rice to soften the flavour. Pure food may be too strong.

Introduce one food at a time so you know if they're allergic. Give them a mixture of foods and you won't know which the problem is!

People think starting with evening meals is best to fill babies up. But if you give them something new and they have a reaction to it, you won't know if they're asleep.

'I always wondered why babies spend so much time
sucking their thumbs. Then I tasted baby food.'
Robert Orben

Preventing Fussy Eating by Kate Barlow
Parenting Consultant and mother of three. She offers online/ personal advice and support to parents to solve their parenting issues. She has developed successful methods to deal with routine, eating, sleeping, behavioural and toilet training issues. She regularly writes parenting technique blogs for magazines and websites, including her own website www.theparentconsultancy.com

Lack of appetite, control and transitions are the most common reasons for fussy eating. Children's appetites vary depending on growth, activity and development.

Sharing mealtimes, allowing your child to feel in control, eating the same food, respecting your child's appetite and allowing him to build an appetite between meals will result in relaxed, sociable mealtimes. Provide opportunities for tasty/healthy/nutritional snacks and drinks, they're important for little tummies to bridge the gap between meals. From 1 year babies no longer need 'milk feeds', encourage your baby to drink from a cup to avoid filling up from comfort sucking on a bottle.

'There is no influence so powerful as that of the mother.'
Sarah Josepha Hale

Introducing Food by Charlie Plunkett
Mum to a gorgeous little boy called Cole and author of 'The True Diaries' series of books. www.charlieplunkett. co.uk

Your child's first taste of food is a momentous occasion, even though it will most likely be bland baby rice that could easily double as wallpaper adhesive - ironically as that is where most of it will end up getting flicked! Progressing to a vast array of puréed vegetables and fruits, some of which will be popular and others will have your baby gurning. For baby-led weaning giving whole pieces of fruit and vegetables will encourage motor skills and co-ordination. Avocado, cucumber and banana were Cole's favourites, so much so that the next thing he sampled was vegan avocado ice-cream!

'Green leafy happiness and cherry-red life,
bursting with seeds.'
Terri Guillemets

The Joys of Weaning by Lisa Wildgoose
A single mother of identical twin girls. www.twinstiaras
andtantrums.com

When weaning babies make sure you have plenty of
EVERYTHING! Bowls, spoons, bibs and patience!
Make sure you have numerous packs of baby wipes to
hand, a vacuum cleaner that will last the distance, and a
mop with more than two tassels attached. Be prepared,
all of the above will get a battering.

There will be food where you never thought food
could go. It'll be up your walls, trodden into your
favourite shag pile carpet and ingrained in your sofa.
Every item of clothing you wear will bear a distinct
orange stain that'll never be removed…

You've been warned!

'If evolution really works, how come mothers only
have two hands?' Milton Berle

Why We Love Baby Led Weaning by Sarah Naylor
Mother to Matthew aged two. She blogs at www.
craftyroo.wordpress.com

It's so easy. From six months we gave Matthew a bit of
whatever we were having for our meals. Before this, he
would grumble during mealtimes, he just wanted to be
involved! After that, he just ate. It's messy, but nothing a
few wipes can't sort out. He eats a huge range of food

now rarely refusing anything and regularly eats large portions. He loves joining in at mealtimes. I'd encourage anyone who is about to wean to try it! Trust yourself and your baby; as long as you eat a balanced diet they will learn nothing but good habits.

'The best thing you can give children,
next to good habits, are good memories.'
Sydney J. Harris

Tom Loves Cheerios by J.M. Worgan
Mother to two young boys. Her youngest son has Autistic Spectrum Disorder. Author of 'Life on the Spectrum. The Preschool Years. Getting the Help and Support You Need'. Available from Amazon. www.goodreads.com/JMWorgan

Tom would eat Cheerios all day if he could, he loves to crunch them. He does not like milk on them and he eats using his fingers. All his food is dry with the exception of bananas. He likes his food to be put on his plate the same way every time. The fish fingers are cut in half and placed on one side with the smiley faces, or tubby toast as Tom likes to name them, on the other side. Any deviation from this and he will not eat them. Why is this you may ask? My Tom is autistic.

'Carrots do something for children's vision. Kids can
spot carrots no matter how you disguise them.'
Anon

Food from Fields by Sarah Wood
Mum of three and blogger at www.mumofthreeworld. blogspot.com

'Daddy, I don't much like food from fields' my daughter announced at the table. And what poisonous 'food from fields' were we trying to feed her? CORN ON THE COB.

It's the same as sweetcorn from a tin, which she will eat, but a bit nicer. To food from fields you can add food from trees, food from under the ground, spicy food, food from foreign countries and any food that is mixed up and includes sauce. The only food my kids really like is food from cows or food processed to within an inch of its life then frozen.

'In retrospect, it was only a matter of time before the Family Dinner passed into history and fast foods took over. I knew its days were numbered the day our youngest propped my mouth open with a fork and yelled into it, "I want a cheeseburger and two fries and get it right this time." I just didn't serve meals with show business pizzazz.' Erma Bombeck, Family: The Ties that Bind and Gag!

Fussy Eating by Helen Neale
A lapsed business analyst, now mum to two lovely, but challenging kids. She runs a parenting advice and reward charts business, KiddyCharts www.kiddycharts.com as well as regularly doing freelance writing for the parenting media, including Britmums, Small Steps Magazine and MumsClub.

Mealtimes are not meant to be a battle. Try to have rules that are simple and they will be a much more pleasurable experience:

1. Eat as much as mummy says is OK, then you can have pudding.

2. If you get down and play, dinner is over.
3. If you don't eat that, there is no alternative.

Three simple rules. Stick to them and your child will know you are serious. Remain calm about the three rules, and you'll be surprised how easy mealtimes can become.

Don't let them become a battleground. Your toddler will always want to win!

'As a child my family's menu consisted
of two choices: take it, or leave it.'
Buddy Hackett

Speech

'Words can be found by a child and an adult bending down and looking together under the grass or at the skittering crabs in the tidal pool.'
Anon

First Words by Charlie Plunkett.
Mum to a gorgeous little boy called Cole and author of 'The True Diaries' series of books. www.charlieplunkett. co.uk

'Da, da, da, da daddy' says my husband. Cole gazes up to him and replies 'ma, ma, ma,ma!' I suppress a giggle, they have been talking like this for a few minutes now and we are no closer to getting the magical words 'daddy' out of our little boy. 'He knows who keeps him fed,' I say patting my chest, 'although I did think it was more common for a baby to form a da word before a ma one.' Dave leaves the room to put the kettle on and Cole stares after him 'Da da da daddy!' he exclaims.

'Ma-ma does everything for the baby, who responds by saying Da-da first.' Mignon McLaughlin, The Second Neurotic's Notebook, 1966

Fab Vocab by Tasha Harrison
Mum of two and author of 'Package Deal', 'Hot Property' and 'Pearls'. When she has time, she also blogs at www.tashaharrison.com

I miss the days when my daughters were little and would come up with some hilarious words, such as 'melmet' (helmet) and 'fuman beans' (human beings).

Once, we were doing a quiz on a long car journey. I asked my youngest, then four, to name three types of bird.

'Peacock, seagull and...' she struggled to think, 'chibbin.'

'You mean chicken?' I said.

'No, chibbin.'

'What's a chibbin?'

'You know!' she said, getting annoyed. 'It's grey - there's one!' She pointed out the car window to a pigeon on the pavement. We had a good laugh, and we still call them chibbins.

'(My son's) only got two words: 'car' and 'map'. I'm slightly worried he's trying to escape. If his next word is 'passport' we are in serious trouble!' Michael McIntyre

Funny Things Children Say by Charlie Plunkett
Mum to a gorgeous little boy called Cole and author of 'The True Diaries' series of books. www.charlieplunkett. co.uk

We were at a 3 year old's birthday party when the topic of conversation moved to the funny things children say. One mummy commented that her daughter had stated 'When I grow up I hope I have a big bottom just like yours mummy!' Whilst a dad said he'd been alarmed when he picked his daughter up from nursery to hear her say 'Daddy I have sore nipples!' after a short pause she reconsidered 'Oh no, not nipples, knuckles!' As I applied sun cream to Cole he looked in horror at his arms and gasped 'Oh no mummy, I'm white!'

'Children seldom misquote. In fact, they usually repeat word for word what you shouldn't have said.'
Author Unknown

Explaining Heaven to a 3 year Old by Sally Littlestone
An insomniac, stay at home mum to two gorgeous children, a son aged 5 and daughter aged 3 and one pretty phenomenal husband. Found blogging about crafts and dreams at www.pressiesbypebbles.com

When they were younger we told our children that their grandparents were up in the stars and gradually bought in the word Heaven.

Mr P took our daughter (3) swimming, on the way home she said "I love going swimming Daddy because it's where I'm close to Grandpa and Granny."

My husband was a bit confused said "Why do you think that? They're in Heaven." She replied, "Mummy said that they're in the water." which lead to him being really confused so he asked her to explain what I had actually said and she replied "Mummy said that they dived!!"

'There's nothing that can help you understand your beliefs more than trying to explain them to an inquisitive child.'
Frank A. Clark

Out of the Mouths of Babes by Charlie Plunkett
Mum to a gorgeous little boy called Cole and author of 'The True Diaries' series of books. www.charlieplunkett. co.uk

Waiting at the pedestrian crossing Cole suddenly shouts out 'Naughty poo poo!' I glance around but can't see anything disgusting in our path. 'Poo poo?' I question 'Yes naughty poo poo (people) crossing before the green man!' he replies.

'Oink oink' Cole does his best pig impression. 'Are you pretending to be a piggy?' I ask. 'Yes and mummy, why do you sleep like a piggy?'

'Up yours!' Cole proudly says as he comes out of school 'Pardon?' I say 'Up yours mummy. It's what one of my friends says, it means goodbye.' I think/hope he meant to say adios!

'You know your children are growing up when they start asking questions that have answers.'
John Plomp

Problems Problems by Ruth-less Shanks
Mum to Ray, Arnie and Mini. Ruth started writing again when her Dad had a health scare and came to stay. Once he was better, he was kicked out (joke), but she carried

on writing about trying to be a better daughter, sister, partner, mother, yada, yada in her blog found here. www.grandadcametotea.wordpress.com

Speech therapy is in the same building as sexual health. In another life, I have removed my knickers here. Speech therapy is equally humiliating.

When I was demanding these sessions, I thought just by attending Arnie would pronounce: "The Rain in Spain" perfectly. Now I know classes are just another step on a wong and linding load. Arnie's Ks sound like Ts and his Ds like Fs. Which makes his yelling "kitty duck" excruciating. The lessons are hard. I am resentful at our struggle.

Although, after, when he asks for "Tiss and tuddle". I think, Sorry, I will try better.

'Real mothers know that a child's growth is not measured by height or years or grades... It is marked by the progression of Mama to Mommy to Mother.'
Anon

Why? By Charlie Plunkett
Mum to a gorgeous little boy called Cole and author of 'The True Diaries' series of books. www.charlieplunkett. co.uk

'What's that?' Cole asks
'It's my bra.' I reply
'What's it for?'
'Erm, to keep my boobs warm.'
'Why doesn't daddy wear a bra?'

'Well daddies don't have boobs that need support.'
'What's support?'
'It means my bra keeps my boobs in place.'
'Why?'
'Erm, if mummy doesn't wear a bra her boobs will be droopy.'
'What's droopy mean mummy?'
'Droopy means my boobs are hanging down and don't look perky.'
'What's perky?'
'Erm...'
'Mummy I don't have boobs do I?'
'No you don't.'
'But I do have nipples.'
'That's right, you do.'
'Why?'
I'm dressing in the bathroom tomorrow!

'A child can ask questions that a wise man cannot answer.'
Author Unknown

A Fish Called Papa by Helen Braid
Helen lives on the West Coast of Scotland with her husband, boy and baby girl. She works as a graphic designer, makes jewellery and loves to write. You can read more from her blog www.allatseascotland.blogspot.co.uk

In the garden of the restaurant with the view to Arran, I asked the nearly 5 year old if he thought he could swim to the island. "No Mummy" came the reply "Sharks might eat me". He gazed over the water as a new response to my query entered his mind.

"Papa could swim to Arran" he informed me with the simplistic certainty of the very young.

Nearby, within earshot and watching from the terrace, the only non-swimmer of the group - my father and papa to my clever boy - flexed his imaginary fins and filled his gills with pride.

'To the world you may be one person, but to one person you may be the world.'
Heather Cortez

What Four Year Olds Might Worry About by Ruth-less Shanks
Mum to Ray, Arnie and Mini. Ruth started writing again when her Dad had a health scare and came to stay. Once he was better, he was kicked out (joke), but she carried on writing about trying to be a better daughter, sister, partner, mother, yada, yada in her blog found here. www.grandadcametotea.wordpress.com

Arnie is changing into his Spiderman pyjamas.

"The end of the world is not soon?" He grips my hand. I connect the question with Grandad's poor health.

"When will it be?"

"Never."

I tell husband that Arnie is worried about Grandad. Grandad used to play ball, push the swing or make playdough superheroes. Perhaps Arnie, our emotional, intuitive boy, senses the end of an era.

It isn't until later, that husband says, "When Arnie was eating, he spilled some spaghetti. I said, 'It isn't the end of the world...' Do you think it's that?"

'Children aren't really interested in your views on the world. You know, they have their own questions, like, 'What is the name for the space in between the bits that stick out on a comb?' Dylan Moran

They Don't Warn You About That In Antenatal Classes!
by Victoria Pearson
Victoria lives behind a keyboard, surrounded by the chaos being married with three children, a dog and a very clumsy cat creates. When she isn't running around screaming, "Be careful" or picking up after someone she is generally to be found writing stories. www.victoria-pearson.webs.com

I thought nothing my kids could do would shock or embarrass me. I had seen it all.

From my daughter aged three asking me in her loudest voice on a crowded bus whether "that person there" (pointing) was a man or a lady, to coming out of a doctor's appointment to find my eleven year old roaring with laughter at the word "erection" in a leaflet he had found about puberty, much to the disgust of all in the waiting room. But nothing compares to having to walk into a pharmacy and ask for worming tablets for your kids. Nice.

'There are only two things a child will share willingly - communicable diseases and his mother's age.'
Benjamin Spock, Dr. Spock's Baby and Child Care, 1945

Parenthood

*'Parenthood is the passing of a baton, followed by
a lifelong disagreement as to who dropped it.'*
Robert Brault

Changes by Sam Coleman
Writer, blogger and stumbling father to a little girl way
ahead of her time and often ahead of him. He is as lost
in the world as you are. You'll find him muttering at
www.dustandlove.wordpress.com

Everything changes. Lack of sleep, lack of time and an
encompassing, paralysing collection of fears all add up
to significant changes in your relationship. You both
invest every nuance of your being into your child. That's
because you're both scared.

You're both scared you're not doing enough. That in
itself is the measure of a good parent. I love my wife more
than I ever have. I have never been this happy. I have never
been this insecure and unsure of myself. I am experiencing
the zenith and the nadir of my own consciousness. I guess
that's what love is.

*'Your children are not your children. They are the sons
and daughters of life's longing for itself. They come
through you, but not from you. And though they are with*

you, yet they belong not to you. You may give them your love but not your thoughts. For they have their own thoughts. You may house their bodies but not their souls, For their souls dwell in the house of tomorrow, which you can not visit, not even in your dreams. You may strive to be like them but, seek not to make them like you. For life goes not backward, nor tarries with yesterday.'
Kahlil Gibran

The Club by Charlie Plunkett
Mum to a gorgeous little boy called Cole and author of 'The True Diaries' series of books. www.charlieplunkett. co.uk

I've never been one for clubs, my shoes were never shiny enough for Brownies and I was useless at marching in the Girl Guides. The pregnancy club was pretty cool, other ladies to compare bumps and maladies with but nothing can beat the club I'm now a member of 'Parenthood.'

Friends made at breastfeeding clubs are friends for life. On a larger scale I feel connected to all parents. We may "parent" differently but we have one thing in common, we are navigating parenthood the best we can and learning on the job. I'm signed up as a lifelong member!

'The trouble with learning to parent on the job is that your child is the teacher.'
Robert Brault

My Children by Meghan Fenn
Author of 'Bringing up Brits' and mum to three children. www.bringingupbrits.co.uk

A first child is a triumph.

A second child is a blessing.

A third child is a family's treasure.

My first child is my pride and joy, my second is my angel and my third is and always will be my baby, my last, a little piece of immortality and sweetness, the one we all watch over and cherish. Through the hard and fast times of parenthood, amid the laughter and kisses, the tears and the hurt, we sometimes have moments of purity and clarity delivered inevitably by the most innocent and vulnerable, and with this, we know true love.

'The first child is made of glass, the second porcelain, the rest of rubber, steel and granite.'
Richard J. Needham

Letting Go of Perfection Nina Badzin
Mom of four, has published essays and short stories in various publications. Find her here at www.ninabadzin. com

The perfect parent doesn't exist, which means we can stop trying to remake ourselves in the image of that mythical creature. We parents drive ourselves crazy trying to make all the right choices. Cloth diapers! Organic food! Master every sport before the age of five! Learn another language! The options for "giving our kids the best" are truly endless, but the only "best" they need is our love and support.

Personally I find it a relief to know that parenthood is not a race or a magic formula.

For better or worse, there are no magic ingredients other than love.

'Self-esteem is the real magic wand that can form a
child's future. A child's self-esteem affects every
area of her existence, from friends she chooses,
to how well she does academically in school,
to what kind of job she gets, to even the person
she chooses to marry.'
Stephanie Martson, The Magic of Encouragement

The Guilty Parent by Lisa Wildgoose
A single mother of identical twin girls. www.twinstiaras
andtantrums.com

Being a parent is about always doing the best you can for
your child, but still managing to feel like you haven't
done enough!

You will love your child unconditionally from the
moment they are born. You will change an obscene
amount of stinky nappies. You will mop their fevered
brow when they're sick. You will hold them tight and
wipe away their tears when their sad. You will do
whatever it takes to make them happy. You will stand by
them no matter what...

But make one mistake and you will carry that guilt
around for a whole lifetime!

'The central struggle of parenthood is to let our
hopes for our children outweigh our fears.'
Ellen Goodman

The Playground by Charlie Plunkett
Mum to a gorgeous little boy called Cole and author of
'The True Diaries' series of books. www.charlieplunkett.
co.uk

It was a beautiful day in September. The unseasonably warm sunshine shone through the autumnal colours of the trees surrounding the playground. I was supporting Cole as he sat on his favourite springy wooden elephant. Glancing around I spotted a dad pushing his giggling daughter on a swing, doting grandparents helping twin boys build sandcastles and a mum was waiting at the bottom of the slide for her little girl. Every adult was 100% focused on their child and the entire playground felt like a magical place. There was nowhere on earth I would rather have been in that moment.

'Tarry a moment to watch the chaos of a playground,
crayola-colored shirts of running children,
all trying out their wings.'
Dr. SunWolf

Patience by Andy Holloman
Dad, Hubby, and Tall Tale Construction Specialist. He is also certified cat herder, keeping all three of them (ages 14, 12, and 9) headed in the right direction. His wife of 20 years is a talented assistant and tolerates his wide array of foibles. He is also a social media goofball, proof of which can be found at his website www.andyholloman.com

Be patient.
Like all new endeavours, becoming a good parent is a learning process, albeit very much an "on-the-job" process. The pressures are overwhelming and easily wear down even the hardiest of souls. Take it slow. Ask for help. Combined with learning, you are regularly forced to give up sleep and make decisions that you simply have

no experience with. But you will. The wisdom will come to you. Your child will help you and so will loving people around you. Patience with yourself is vital. Wouldn't your child want you to be patient with yourself? I know they would.

'Have patience with all things, but chiefly have patience with yourself. Do not lose courage in considering your own imperfections, but instantly set about remedying them - every day begin the task anew.'
Saint Francis De Sales

Words of Wisdom by Fiona Cambouropoulos
Wife to Farmer Nick and Mummy to six children, including triplets; living the good life at Coombe Mill, their Holiday Farm in Cornwall. Blogs the behind the scenes of farm life and parenting and promotes outdoor play for children through Country Kids website www.coombemill.com/blog

Put your relationship first, kids need love, stability, security and family time. To discipline is to love. Take the easy short term option with kids at your peril! Look long term in sleep routines, eating habits and manners. Have a routine in the early days but don't be a slave to it. Encourage freedom and independence; we all learn from our mistakes. Working Mums need good child care, this is not detrimental to your children so cut the guilt. Finally kids are like puppies, they need daily exercise; get them outdoors for your benefit and theirs! Above all enjoy parenthood.

'If you want children to keep their feet on the ground,
put some responsibility on their shoulders.'
Abigail Van Buren

Good Advice by Stephanie Cracknell
Founder of Mathemagical, making maths fun for
pre-school children, winner of the 'Woman in Education' award and mum of two lovely children. www.
mathemagical.co.uk

So what have I gleamed
About the joys of parenthood?
Any pearls of wisdom?
Advice to give that's good?
The biggest lesson I've learnt
Over five wondrous years
Is don't take "good advice"
It only leads to tears
Some say "always co-sleep"
Some say "definitely not"
Some say "carry all day in a sling"
Some say "in a cot!"
I've never been so confused
So this is what I'd say to you
My advice, for what it's worth
Every child is different
By temperament and look
You know your child better
Than any nurse or book!

'There is no way to be a perfect mother,
and a million ways to be a good one.'
Jill Churchill

Toddlers, First Steps
and Toilet Training

'When my kids become wild and unruly, I use a nice,
safe playpen. When they're finished, I climb out.'
Erma Bombeck

Baby Proofing by Charlie Plunkett
Mum to a gorgeous little boy called Cole and author of
'The True Diaries' series of books. www.charlieplunkett.
co.uk

When Cole started crawling and cruising we realised
it was time to take a good look at our home from an
inquisitive toddlers point of view. So... We moved our
ornaments and treasures out of reach, put a magnetic
lock on the cupboard under the sink, erected a stair gate
and lowered the base of his crib so he couldn't topple out.

But... The thing that still to this day makes me smile
is my husband's ingenious idea to prevent any accidents
involving our toddlers head with the hard granite of our
kitchen worktop. A nappy taped to the corner!

'I think, at a child's birth, if a mother could ask
a fairy godmother to endow it with the most
useful gift, that gift would be curiosity.'
Eleanor Roosevelt

Those First Unaided Steps by Charlie Hughes
Mum of 2 beautiful, spirited girls, freelance writer who also blogs at www.sophiaschoiceuk.blogspot.co.uk and www.madmummymusings.blogspot.co.uk

There are many milestones your little one will achieve along their journey as a child but one of the most exciting is when they take those first unaided steps. From complete dependence to independence. Wow, what a feeling it is as they precariously take one step, then two in your direction, doing their best Orangutan impression with the biggest grin on their face as they finally collapse into your loving, safe and welcoming arms. What a moment that is. And it's just as amazing the second time around. Oh the wonder and joy of little people. Bottle those moments forever.

> *'The finest inheritance you can give to a
> child is to allow it to make its own way,
> completely on its own feet.'*
> *Isadora Duncan*

First 3 Steps by Charlie Plunkett
Mum to a gorgeous little boy called Cole and author of 'The True Diaries' series of books. www.charlieplunkett.co.uk

It was a beautiful autumn afternoon when Cole took his first steps unaided. He had a determined glint in his eyes as he eased himself to standing and precariously tottled forwards a step before crumpling down on the lawn of The Royal Pavilion Gardens.

He tried again and this time managed a step and a half before his legs gave way.

We were so engaged in this momentous occasion we didn't notice an audience of foreign exchange students watching on. As Cole took a triumphant 3 steps they all burst into rapturous applause, while we practically clucked with parental pride.

*'I can only imagine where these tiny feet will go
in their lifetime. My only hope is that they
never forget the way home.'*
Candice G

Toddlerhood by Michelle Lee
An entrepreneur, blogger, writer, occasional amateur photographer and most importantly Mommy to a dangerously cute 2 ½ year old. Mostly found styling bump and beyond with a chic, modern collection at www.keungzai.com

When he starts rolling around the supermarket floor screaming, know that we, parents, have all been there. Know that you aren't the first parent to experience your little angel unmask The Toddler Rage in public; on the side pavement, in the shop, in the park, in the car park, on the train, in the car, at the dentist...any public space is applicable to the unveiling of The Toddler Rage. Know that this is a phase. He is still the wonderful angel you know. And those warm hugs, kisses and 'I love yous' make your patience and love all the more worthwhile.

*'A two-year-old is kind of like having a blender,
but you don't have a top for it.'*
Jerry Seinfeld

Toddlerdom; a sweet mix of war and peace! By Charlie Hughes
Mum of 2 beautiful, spirited girls, freelance writer who also blogs at www.sophiaschoiceuk.blogspot.co.uk and www.madmummymusings.blogspot.co.uk

Toddlers. They're certainly a law unto themselves. You can compare them to teenagers really; headstrong, hot-headed, misunderstood! That said, this period of time is so much fun. They're constantly learning: to walk, to talk, to play, experiencing new things around them. Empower their confidence to explore this amazing, world. Try not to instil too much caution. Give them as much free rein to be themselves as you can. Their "free spirit" and "joie de vivre" can be intoxicating if you immerse yourself in the time you spend with them. Toddlers laugh, a lot, so spend your time laughing with them.

'When I pick up one of my children and cuddle them, all the strain and stress of life temporarily disappears. There is nothing more wonderful than motherhood and no one will ever love you as much as a small child.'
Nicola Horlick

10 Potty Training Tips by Lisa Wildgoose
A single mother of identical twin girls. www.twinstiaras andtantrums.com

1. Perseverance... Something I lack!
2. Bribery... Not PC, but worked for me!
3. Cheap pants... Buy as many as possible!

4. Don't call pull ups pants... When the girls started wearing pull ups, I called them pants. Imagine their confusion?
5. Use a timer... set a timer every 15 minutes to remind you.
6. Pirate Pete... This book is renowned in the world of potty training.
7. Stay home... Or be within a metre radius of a toilet.
8. Once in pants, stay in pants... It will click eventually.
9. Patience... 5 toilet dashes while trying to eat a hot lunch is normal...
10. EAT COLD FOOD... See above!

'Parenting is a stage of life's journey where the milestones come about every fifty feet.'
Robert Brault

A Conversation with my 3 Year Old by Charlie Plunkett Mum to a gorgeous little boy called Cole and author of 'The True Diaries' series of books. www.charlieplunkett.co.uk

'So whenever you think you want to do a wee or a poo, as the book says, you put your botty on the potty'. 'Why?' my little boy asks. 'Well otherwise it will go all over your clothes and the floor'. 'Why?' he replies again. 'You don't want to do a wee on the floor do you? Mummy and daddy don't do that.' This elicits a giggle followed by a long list of places he doesn't want to do a wee or a poo including his tractor; racing car, bed, the TV, sofa, rug, or it would appear his potty!

'Usually the triumph of my day is, you know,
everybody making it to the potty.'
Julia Roberts

Smelly Old Pot by Mary Dudley
Mum to three 'grown-up' daughters and grandma to
eight wonderful grandchildren.

What a pot! Waste of time sitting a baby on a pot to
perform, it's just luck if they go.

As speech develops and when baby can talk take them
to the toilet and let them sit on a small inset seat. Their
bladders are still growing so I did not expect too much
but by two and a half they will achieve this. They need
to be able to tell you and also climb onto the toilet. Who
wants to carry a smelly old pot around? The toilet is
where it goes so that's where they should do it.

'Patience and perseverance have a magical effect before
which difficulties disappear and obstacles vanish.'
John Quincy Adams

My 100 Words on Potty Training by Helen Neale
A lapsed business analyst, now mum to two lovely, but
challenging kids. She runs a parenting advice and reward
charts business called KiddyCharts at www.kiddycharts.
com as well as regularly doing freelance writing for
the parenting media, including Britmums, Small Steps
Magazine and MumsClub.

Wait. Be patient

That's actually three words. However they are all
you really need to make potty training a success. Potty

training is not a trial. It is not something that we should be dreading as parents. All good things come to those who wait, they say. So why do we parents find it so hard to wait for this good thing to happen? Nappies are smelly.

But they are not as smelly as wee covered clothes, poo-filled pants, and stained sofas! So wait until they train themselves. That way, you will have a much easier and less soggy life!

'Learn the art of patience. Apply discipline to your thoughts when they become anxious over the outcome of a goal. Impatience breeds anxiety, fear, discouragement and failure. Patience creates confidence, decisiveness, and a rational outlook, which eventually leads to success.'
Brian Adams

Yellow Potty by Charlie Plunkett
Mum to a gorgeous little boy called Cole and author of 'The True Diaries' series of books.www.charlieplunkett. co.uk

Day one and buoyed with the excitement of a reward chart and stickers we are off to a flying start with a wee, a poo and another wee all making the magnificent yellow potty. Day two and we replicate day one's success. Days three and four are not so great, I spend half the day worrying that he is holding it in while we are out, only to miss catching anything in the potty when we return home. By day five I'm seriously considering putting him back in his pull-ups but realise that perseverance and patience is what is required.

'Perseverance is not a long race. It is many short races one after another.'
W. Elliot

Potty Training Hell by Lisa Wildgoose
A single mother of identical twin girls. www.twinstiaras
andtantrums.com

Our first day of potty training was hell! Four accidents before 11 am (one really messy), and I was nearly running back to the nappy drawer again... Thankfully my friend was on hand to support me in this momentary lapse of confidence. Her wise words "it can't possibly get any worse, therefore it can only get better" were a much needed positive view on the whole episode. So I persevered, and she was right it did get better, with only a few more hiccups that week. 4 months later I have one completely dry twin! The other...well that's another story altogether!

'In a household of toddlers and pets, we discover this rule of thumb about happy families - that they are least two-thirds incontinent.'
Robert Brault

Nursery

*'The formative period for building character for
eternity is in the nursery. The mother is queen
of that realm and sways a scepter more potent
than that of kings or priests.'*
Author Unknown

Childcare by Ruth-less Shanks
Mum to Ray, Arnie and Mini. Ruth started writing again
when her Dad had a health scare and came to stay. Once
he was better, he was kicked out (joke), but she carried
on writing about trying to be a better daughter, sister,
partner, mother, yada, yada in her blog at her website.
www.grandadcametotea.wordpress.com

Sometimes when Mini and I are snuggling, she says,
"Pretend to be Becky," (her key-worker at nursery) and
what she is saying is, be more fun.

"Do you mind?" asks husband warily.

"No it's ok," I say because I know great childcare is
not to be sneezed at and besides, Becky is lovely.

Still, I don't mention that the last picture Mini made
for him was originally for Becky.

Smarties helped persuade her otherwise. And I don't
tell him that yesterday after she was told off, I cuddled her
and she mumbled into my hair: "I want my play school."

*'On the way to preschool, the doctor had left her
stethoscope on the car seat, and her little girl picked it
up and began playing with it. Be still, my heart, she
thought, my daughter wants to follow in my footsteps!
Then the child spoke into the instrument:
'Welcome to McDonald's. May I take your order?'*
Anon

Nursery by Charlie Plunkett
Mum to a gorgeous little boy called Cole and author of 'The
True Diaries' series of books. www.charlieplunkett.co.uk

Sporting a new haircut, clutching his book bag and
rucksack and Cole is ready for the first day of nursery.
I'm not sure I'm ready though, it seems like only
yesterday my little boy was a baby and yet here he is
taking his first steps towards independence.

We arrive and are greeted by the smiling faces of
the nursery staff. One of them informs me that on the
morning's agenda they will be making pear crumble
from the fruit of a small tree in the playground, 'Do
stay' she says. I don't need asking twice and remain until
Christmas!

'Being a mother has made my life complete.'
Darcy Bussell

Nursery: (unfortunately) the best day of my child's life by
Louise Hamilton
A proud mummy to Jennifer who at 2 ½ already runs
rings around both her parents. She likes to think she
spends her days being a domestic goddess but usually
she has cake mixture and glitter in her unkempt hair.

She is writing a series of books about motherhood.
www.mummy-diaries.co.uk

Jennifer's first day at nursery started off great, we had already done a stay and play session so this was her first proper day where I dropped her off and hid round the corner anticipating the floods of tears. I felt slightly hurt when I peeked round the door frame to a perfectly contented child covered in paint laughing with one of the staff. As I was leaving I pretended to everyone that I was totally fine with her being so blasé about the situation, I went and sat in my car and cried for a long time - emotional.

'Sometimes the strength of motherhood
is greater than natural laws.'
Barbara Kingsolver

Young Children and Behaviour

'Childhood is the world of miracle or of magic:
it is as if creation rose luminously out of the night,
all new and fresh and astonishing. Childhood
is over the moment things are no longer
astonishing. When the world gives you a
feeling of "déjà vu," when you are used
to existence, you become an adult.'
Eugene Ionesco, Present Past / Past Present

The Mysteries of Childhood by Lisa Wildgoose
A single mother of identical twin girls. www.twinstiaras
andtantrums.com

What is it about puddles that attract children so much?
They're cold, they're wet and they're muddy! So why do
they take great delight in jumping in them so hard that
they can actually soak themselves through to their pants?
When I deliver mine to school in torrential rain; when it's
so miserable that it makes them squeal when the rain hits
their little faces, they love it and will still jump into every
deep puddle that they come across... Where is the logic
in that? It is one of those mysteries of childhood that
I will never figure out!

'Puddle: a small body of water that draws other
small bodies wearing new shoes into it.'
Unknown

Kids at Weddings by James Smith.
Father of three wonderful boys. When he finds a spare
moment he attempts to write fiction. He is a founding
member of a short story group, who publish seasonal
collections to raise money for charity. www.short
storiesgroup.blogspot.co.uk and blogs at www.jamessm
1th.wordpress.com

Children make weddings. They provide parents with
distractions during those boring bits and give the DJ
something to do at 6 pm.

At their grandfather's wedding, all my sons were the
poster boys for charm and cuteness. During the evening
my middle son happily danced with the old ladies who
couldn't find anyone to talk to, whilst gulping down
orange juice from the free bar. All great until a rather cross
looking elderly lady returned my son to our table. He had
a green face and she had vomit on her shoulder - guess he'd
been drinking someone else's discarded "orange juice".

'All of us have moments in our lives that test
our courage. Taking children into a house
with a white carpet is one of them.'
Erma Bombeck

My Child is not 'Naughty' by J.M. Worgan
Mother to two young boys. Her youngest son has
Autistic Spectrum Disorder. Author of 'Life on the

Spectrum. The Preschool Years. Getting the Help and Support You Need'. Available from Amazon. www. goodreads.com/JMWorgan

My child is on the autistic spectrum, they do not 'see' the world as you or I do, they see things in a totally different way and sometimes because of this become overwhelmed. There is too much noise, the lights flicker, or there are too many images to process. This often results in a 'meltdown' where the child reacts physically and verbally to what is distressing them. This is a child who needs help and empathy. A child who needs understanding and protection. This is not a naughty child. This child could be your child. This child is my Tom.

> *'Autism (with a capital "A") to me, says that I accept my child wholly. I celebrate his differences and his quirky-ness. I advocate diversity. I try to empower him. I am proud of his successes, no matter how small they seem. I hope he holds onto the compassion he has in his heart into adulthood. I do not think he needs "fixing". I am proud that he is my son, and sometimes I am humbled by that very same thought'*
> *Mommy-dearest at The Quirk Factor: Resistance Is Futile.*

Children's Behaviour by Lisa Wildgoose
A single mother of identical twin girls. www.twinstiaras andtantrums.com

Don't you love grandparents? They always brag how good grandchildren are around them! I was once told that how children behave around others is a true reflection of their behavioural skills.

For instance, if they behave well around others, it means you've taught them well and they're well behaved, well-mannered children.

Well to be honest I don't care what mine are like around others I want them to be good around me! I am the one that has made these the well behaved children that people say they are. Yet all I get is the endless arguing and fighting!

'Hot dogs always seem better out than at home; so do French-fried potatoes; so do your children.'
Mignon McLaughlin

Gaining Co-operation from Our Children by Naomi Richards
Author of 'The Parent's Toolkit' www.thekidscoach.org.uk and mum to 2 boys.

There's another way to ask your children to do something rather than nagging - a way they will be more receptive and cooperative with. Children like it when you ask them to do something and you also explain to them why you are asking them. It also helps if you give them a time for when they have to complete the task if the ask is task orientated. They will then know what they have to do and when they have to do it by. By giving children a reason for our request they will be more inclined to do it.

'The child supplies the power but the parents have to do the steering.'
Benjamin Spock

Reward Charts by Helen Neale
A lapsed business analyst, now mum to two lovely, but challenging kids. She runs a parenting advice and reward charts business, KiddyCharts www.kiddycharts.com as well as regularly doing freelance writing for the parenting media, including Britmums, Small Steps Magazine and MumsClub.

My kids aren't perfect. Are anybody's? Perhaps the Nike-wearing-perfect-make-up- doing mummy at the school gate I aspire to be instead of the last-minute-wet-hair-mummy that I am. However, my kids do understand more about how they are expected to behave thanks to reward charts. The positive way we use them means they're encouraged to feel proud of themselves too. Not proud because we are telling them they should be, but proud because THEY know how well they have done. If you use reward charts positively, you may even get to have that shower, so you don't have wet hair at drop off!

'If you raise your children to feel they can accomplish any goal or task they decide upon, you will have succeeded as a parent and you will have given your child the greatest of blessings.'
Brian Tracy

Bullying by Roxana Rudzik-Shaw (MSc (Dist), BSc (dual hons), MBACP, MBPsS, ACTO)
Psychologist, Counsellor, Clinical Supervisor, Bullying Expert and God-Mother www.rrs.counselling.co.uk

Bullying is an indiscriminate world-wide social phenomenon. Children's 'status' or bullying roles are to some extent informed by their early relationships and attachments, or the lack of them. As with most behaviour, regardless of it being perceived as good or bad, bullying was often learned through reinforcement.

Therefore, parenthood is an important channel for 'modelling' effective relationships, by setting and maintaining clear boundaries, reinforcing a positive mental attitude and embracing individual differences. These ingredients may increase your child's self-awareness, their sense of self-worth, overall wellbeing and be a good foundation to cultivate positive relationships, which minimise negative effects of bullying.

'Parents need to fill a child's bucket of self-esteem so high that the rest of the world can't poke enough holes to drain it dry.'
John Wooden

Parenting

*'You don't really understand human nature unless
you know why a child on a merry- go-round will
wave at his parents every time around - and why
his parents will always wave back.'*
William D. Tammeus

The Greatest Gift by Charlie Plunkett
Mum to a gorgeous little boy called Cole and author of 'The
True Diaries' series of books. www.charlieplunkett.co.uk

Being a parent is a license to see and live the world
through the eyes of your child. It is an excuse to skip in
the street, sing on the bus and blow bubbles in the park.
You get to build sandcastles, play on the swings and try
to fit your bottom down the slide.

Favourite pastimes are standing on drain lids, playing
tractors and rolling on grassy banks. When you are a
parent you have an excuse to have a bag full of snacks
and someone who loves you unconditionally. Being a
parent is the greatest gift in life.

*'One of a parent's best jobs is waiting at
the bottom of a long slide' Dee Ann Stewart
from "What Spock Forgot"*

Parenting by Ellen Arnison
A journalist, writer, blogger, mother of three sons, wife and, occasionally, whole person. She's often found at www.ellenarnison.com

As soon as the test turns blue, you give the world the green light to run your life.

Everyone from your grandmother to the government will know best - after a while your head will spin and you wonder how you ever achieved anything.

Congratulations, you are now a proper parent destined to feel guilty and inadequate whatever you choose. Here's the solution: Ignore it all and know that if you cuddle and read to your child, laugh with them and jump in puddles you are good enough - and none of the rest really matters in the long run.

'There's nothing like a mama-hug.'
Terri Guillemets

Learning to Cope by Joanne Phillips
Author and mother to Lulu aged 4. www.joannephillips. co.uk

It gets easier. This should be a new parent's mantra, especially during the early months. People tell you this all the time, of course, and you think: When? How?

What they don't tell you is that you won't notice it getting easier, because every day brings new challenges, and by the time you are in a position to look back and view the sleepless nights and the tantrums and the feelings of impotence through rose tinted glasses, they no longer seem so bad. So that's the secret - being a parent gets easier because you just learn how to do it.

*'It's not only children who grow. Parents do too.
As much as we watch to see what our children do
with their lives, they are watching us to see what
we do with ours. I can't tell my children to reach
for the sun. All I can do is reach for it, myself.'*
Joyce Maynard

Parenting a Child with Aspergers Syndrome by Claire Louise
Mother of three children, one with Aspergers syndrome and a volunteer SEN advisor. She writes an award winning blog 'A boy with Asperger's' www.aspergersinfo.wordpress.com while unleashing creativity over at 'A mummy of many talents' www.mummyofmanytalents.wordpress.com

As a mother of a child with Asperger's syndrome the best parenting tip I could give you when parenting a child with autism is to get organised. Routines, schedules, visual reward charts, and more, will all make your life that bit easier and your child will be much calmer for it. Children with autism need to know what's coming next.

They often don't like unannounced changes and feel much happier when they are provided a visual timetable for their day. Keep it simple for your child by combining both pictures and words to timetables. Yes it's simple but very effective.

*'If a child is given love, he becomes loving ...
If he's helped when he needs help, he becomes
helpful. And if he has been truly valued
at home ... he grows up secure enough to look
beyond himself to the welfare of others.'*
Dr Joyce Brothers, *Good House Keeping*

Parenting Without Words by Vivien Sabel
Award-winning author of The Blossom Method™ -
The Revolutionary Way To Communicate With Your
Baby From Birth, Psychotherapist and Mum. www.
viviensabel.com

Body language forms a significant part of communication and can be used in positive parenting. Conversely
a lack of awareness can promote feelings of confusion
resulting in low self-esteem. Your children become
accustomed to ALL of you, absorbing you wholly. They
do not filter the spoken word and ignore the language
of the body.

Positive communication with positive faces and more
serious expressions when the need arises will support
growth and development. Be true and this will promote
real and clear communication and a true sense of self,
thus encouraging your children in the development of
empathy. Keep it real!

'Babies need social interactions with loving
adults who talk with them, listen to their babblings,
name objects for them, and give them
opportunities to explore their worlds.'
Sandra Scarr

Taking a Lifelong Learning Approach to Parenting by
Dr Rosina McAlpine
An award-winning educator turning the science of
child development into the art of parenting. Founder of
Inspired Children: life skills for kids in just 15 minutes at
a time. www.inspiredchildren.com

When I first became a mother I was overwhelmed by the enormous responsibility of raising another human being. Holding my sweet boy in my arms, I wondered how I was going to learn everything I needed to know to give him the best possible start in life and the on-going guidance to help him lead a happy, healthy and successful life.

I felt relieved when I realised that I didn't need to know everything right now! Taking a lifelong approach to learning about my child's development and good parenting means I can support his mind, body and spirit as he grows.

'Whenever I held my newborn baby in my arms,
I used to think that what I said and did to him could
have an influence not only on him but on all
whom he met, not only for a day or a month
or a year, but for all eternity - a very challenging
and exciting thought for a mother.'
Rose Kennedy

Nurture by Charmain Zimmerman Brackett
Mother of three, Jessica, 25, Jeremy, 19, and Allie, 17. All three are dancers. Find Charmain's books, 'The Key of Elyon' and 'Elyon's Cipher' at Amazon or visit her website www.charmainzbrackett.com

When my son was 6, we attended a performance of The Nutcracker to see his younger sister's cameo role as a snow angel. He was bored for most of the ballet until Sugar Plum Fairy and her Cavalier came out on stage. The young man effortlessly lifted the dazzling ballerina in an array of graceful poses causing my young son to look at me and say "I want to do that. He's strong."

This Christmas, it's my son's turn to be the Cavalier. Always nurture your children's gifts and don't force them into your mould.

*'Kids: they dance before they learn there
is anything that isn't music.'*
William Stafford

Tragic Heroines by Peter Tye
Dad to three grown-up children one of whom, Zannie, has made him so proud by following in her mother's footsteps by training to become a nurse.

When my daughter Zannie was younger we went to see Les Miserables in London.

Zannie's favourite character was Fantine who tragically dies leaving her young daughter Cosette in the care of Valjean. In Zannie's last year at secondary school she auditioned for a production of Les Miserables and much to her delight was given the part of Fantine. Zannie's heart-felt acting and beautiful singing left us all in tears. The next year in a local production Zannie played Juliet with its famous heart-rending finale. Zannie was so wonderful in both parts, her mum would have been so proud of her.

*'All that I am or ever hope to be,
I owe to my angel Mother.'*
Abraham Lincoln

When your Child is Sick by Charlie Plunkett
Mum to a gorgeous little boy called Cole and author of 'The True Diaries' series of books. www.charlieplunkett.co.uk

There is nothing, worse than being a parent when your child is sick. The feelings of helplessness and wanting to make things better, coupled with recrimination - maybe if we had or hadn't done this he wouldn't be ill. Wishing it was you and not your child throwing up all night, seeing them lethargic and unwell is the worst thing in the world.

But it's all part and parcel of being a parent. It will test your parenting skills to the limit and when it passes it will make you grateful, relieved and determined not to take good health for granted.

'The best medicine in the world is a mother's kiss.'
Anonymous

The Secret of My Success by Stephen C. Spencer
Proud father of Kaitlyn (13) and Evan (9), and the equally-proud husband of their mother, Melissa. When he's not busy parenting (and when is that, exactly?) he's also the author of the increasingly-popular series of thrillers starring ace reporter Paul Mallory...who has no children, for what he considers excellent reasons. www.stephencspencer.com

"First, get a million dollars."

That's Steve Martin's advice to aspiring millionaires, and, when asked to give my views on successful parenting (which isn't often), my answer is analogous to his:

First, get some great kids. I should know, because Kaitlyn and Evan are two of the best there are. I don't remember having much to do with that. Maybe I did, maybe not.

Who can say?

And what next? If you're me, you follow the child-rearing advice of another great comedian, President Harry Truman: Find out what your kids want to do, and then encourage them to do it.

> *'Do not ask that your kids live up to your expectations. Let your kids be who they are, and your expectations will be in breathless pursuit.'*
> *Robert Brault*

Unconditional Love, Sometimes Being a Parent Isn't Easy...by Eileen Stuart
Mum of three, grandma to two adorable little boys. Loves baking, good books, food, shoes and wine, not necessarily in that order! www.thesearegrandmas thoughts.wordpress.com

You raise and nurture them. Protect them, whilst allowing them freedom to practise flying.

You gently tell of trials and pressures they may come across without destroying their innocence.

You hope they make wise choices, best decisions, take the right paths with the right people And when they don't?

When they cause sleepless nights. Endless tears. When they scream they hate you.

When they shout YOU don't love them.

When you love them... but don't like them.

What do you do?

You wait. Quietly. Pray. Hope. Weep silently.

And they come back.

Stronger. Closer. Wiser. Contrite. Weary. Loving. Yours again.

'There are two lasting bequests we can give our children. One is roots. The other is wings.'
Hodding Carter, Jr.

Family

'In family life, be completely present.'
Lao Tzu

Recipe for a Happy Family by Charlie Plunkett
Mum to a gorgeous little boy called Cole and author of 'The
True Diaries' series of books. www.charlieplunkett.co.uk

The main ingredient is love, add a big chunk of happiness
and tickle in. Sprinkle with laughter, compassion and
mutual adoration. Pour in plenty of support and the best
advice you can. Try not to stir, tickle the ingredients some
more instead as this will give the best results. Add some
excellent good health, prosperity and some more love.
Place in a beautiful container, don't rush, take time to
listen and nurture the magnificent family cake you are
baking. Chill by a window overlooking your dream
view. Decorate with passion, joy and magic. Share your
beautiful creation with each other.

'Love makes a family.'
Gigi Kaeser

2 Journeys, 1 Family by Vicki
Adoptive mum to Mini, who's very nearly 6, and birth
mum to Dollop who is 2 ½.

Vicki is also a blogger, and you can read more about her and her family's journey towards help for Mini at www.theboysbehaviour.blogspot.com

No blue line. Disappointment. Next month?
No blue line. Tears. Next month?
No blue line. Desperation. Next month?
No blue line. Heartbreak. Infertile.
Options. Adoption. Family?
Assessment. Approval. Parents!
My son. A joy. Happiness.
Life. Love. Laughter.
Blue line. Shock. Pregnant?
Impossible. Infertile. Adopter.
Scans. Midwives.Tests.
Monitoring. Doctors. Stretch marks.
Shopping. Cot construction. Stretchy leggings.
Nursing bras. Preparing toddler. Choosing names.
Induction. Breaking waters. Contractions.
Epidural. Emergency caesarean section. My daughter.
Breastfeeding. Bottles. Nappies.
Sleep deprivation. Tiny clothes. Total dependence.
Jealousy. Differences. Sadness.
Change. Questions. Attention.
Arguments. Fighting. Sibling rivalry.
Playtime. Protection. Sibling adoration.
Birth. Adoption. Children.
Family. Mine. My family.

*'Biology is the least of what makes
someone a mother.'*
Oprah Winfrey

Childhood Memories by Lisa Wildgoose
A single mother of identical twin girls. www.twinstiaras
andtantrums.com

I love nothing more than taking my children out. I enjoy reliving my youth through their eyes. Doing the things I used to do. That is what having children is all about! It's about being able to find that inner child again, the person I used to be, before the monotony of life wore me down. The fun and the laughter of having my little family around me and the happiness they bring. You learn very quickly in life that you cannot rely on anyone but your family, and I'm looking forward to enjoying mine 100% as they grow up!

'The family. We were a strange little band
of characters trudging through life sharing diseases
and toothpaste, coveting one another's desserts,
hiding shampoo, borrowing money, locking
each other out of our rooms, inflicting pain
and kissing to heal it in the same instant, loving,
laughing, defending, and trying to figure out the
common thread that bound us all together.'
Erma Bombeck

For My Mother - A Very Special Gang by Ellie Stoneley
Ellie is self-employed, loves local, social media, margaritas, technology for good and does consulting. She became a mother, a first time geriatric mother at 47 to Hope now aged 11 months; beautiful, alert and thriving. She is the writer of 'Mush Brained Ramblings' www.crazypregnantperson.com

They are a gang, the two of them, best friends. One 85 ³/₄ and the other 11 months.

Hope and Granby, Granby and Hope. My mother and my girl. They have a special way of communicating, they touch index fingers and they have secret smile.

When she was tiny, first born, Granby sat for hours with Hope fast asleep on her lap, now they play wonderful games together with her teddies and toys, laughing and chatting. I listen just outside the door, happy.

We are so lucky we three to enjoy so much time together, but they are a gang.

'Grandmothers are just "antique" little girls.'
Author Unknown

Family Time by Anna Cahalin
Mum of The Princess and The Pea www.dummy mummy.co.uk

Being mum of two small children is fun, exhausting, exciting, and time-consuming.

The day can go from squeals of delight at playing outside to screams of disgust at being told 'No' within seconds, with a background tune that alternates between screaming, wailing baby and gurgling, happy baby. Quiet time no longer exists. Time to sit down happens only after tea time and bath time, and all evidence of the daily activities tidied away for tomorrow. No more me time. But plenty of family time, which really is more special, more enjoyable and more amazing than any other kind of time.

'The work will wait while you show the child the rainbow,
but the rainbow won't wait while you do the work.'
Patricia Clafford

Getting Back to Basics by Charlie Plunkett
Mum to a gorgeous little boy called Cole and author of 'The
True Diaries' series of books. www.charlieplunkett.co.uk

There is nothing that can beat a good old fashioned
family holiday. It involves packing your entire house into
your car, driving a short enough distance you can pop
home if it rains or your tent blows away and saying bye-
bye to all technology, as there will invariably be no signal
from the field you have pitched your tent in.

What there will be is plenty of fresh air and open
space to play, fun round the campfire and early nights
snuggled up together reading by torchlight and playing
hand shadows. Quality family time and memories made
to treasure forever.

'Have you never, when waves were breaking,
watched children at sport on the beach. With their
little feet tempting the foam-fringe, till with stronger
and further reach. Than they dreamed of, a billow
comes bursting, how they turn and scamper and
screech!' Alfred Austin, A Woman's Apology

The Canal by Sarah Wood
Mum of three and blogger found at www.mumofthree
world.blogspot.com

The kids were going crazy for the ducks swimming
around the canal boat. Suddenly they were screaming.

I went to investigate and saw my daughter, face just visible above the water, with a pink Croc bobbing away from her.

Seeing your daughter's little head surrounded by filthy brown water is not the nicest sight. It's horrible and scary. My first instinct was to grab her, but my exit was blocked. By my eldest. To grab her would knock him in. So I did what anyone would do, screamed for my husband, who instantly hauled her up and into the boat.

'Children in a family are like flowers in a bouquet: there's always one determined to face in an opposite direction from the way the arranger desires.'
Marcelene Cox

Bedtime Story Bliss by Victoria Pearson
Victoria lives behind a keyboard, surrounded by the chaos being married with three children, a dog and a very clumsy cat creates. When she isn't running around screaming, "Be careful" or picking up after someone she is generally to be found writing stories. www.victoria-pearson.webs.com

We are a fairly chaotic family. We have our routines, sure, but none of them are set in stone, bar one. Bedtime stories are a non-negotiable must. Every night, without fail at 7 pm the whole family troops upstairs, gets into Mum and Dad's bed and snuggles down for a good story. We might not all be there for breakfast or dinner or baths, but we are all always together for story time. Even Eldest, who is now 12, still joins us. It is one of those perfect family traditions that has grown over time to be something that defines us.

'Being a parent means never having a minute...
yet always making a moment.'
Michael Nolan

The Family Changing Room by Mark Richards
Mark started writing a weekly column about his children ten years ago. He's gone from nativity plays and party bags to teenage angst, slamming doors and boyfriends he's - wisely - not told about. You can find his 'Best Dad I Can Be' books on the Kindle and follow the battle with his teenage children at www.best dadicanbe.com

Eventually, everyone with children has to face it: the family changing room at the swimming pool.

"Tom, will you please stop trailing that towel along the floor?"

"You've left your goggles? Well go back and get them."

"Ben, wait until we're in the changing room before you take your trunks off."

"No, I don't know which bag your pants are in."

"Rub yourself, darling. If you just stand there we'll be here until Christmas."

"Then you won't get any presents. Father Christmas isn't going to look in the swimming pool."

"Jessica, your mother is naked. Please don't open the door..."

'If your kids are giving you a headache,
follow the directions on the aspirin bottle,
especially the part that says "keep away from
children." Susan Savannah

Extra-Curricular Activities... by Ruth-less Shanks
Mum to Ray, Arnie and Mini. Ruth started writing again
when her Dad had a health scare and came to stay. Once
he was better, he was kicked out (joke), but she carried on
writing about trying to be a better daughter, sister, partner,
mother, yada, yada in her blog. www.grandadcametotea.
wordpress.com

Before I had kids, I had no idea how much time they
would spend at swimming lessons and how much time
I would spend pool-side. The children must learn to
swim and it's my duty to enable them. But it's hot. It
smells. There is the pathos of an abandoned armband,
the way you don't know whether to put the children's
ears in or out the hats and worse, the way you are just
composing a text when they emerge shivering and
needing a wee. One lesson a week: three children: five
years. That's 1,000,000 lengths of my life.

'You can learn many things from children. How much
patience you have, for instance.'
Franklin P. Jones

Birthdays, Christmas
and the Tooth Fairy

'Children will soon forget your presents. They will always remember your presence though.'
Anonymous

Birthdays by Lynsey
A proud Mum with two sons. An energetic, fiery red-headed Toddler and a cheeky eight year old who has Cerebral Palsy and wicked sense of humour. Lynsey writes about parenthood at www.lynseythemotherduck. blogspot.com

Until I had children I did not realise the importance of birthdays to parents. I looked at those throwing extravagant parties for 2 year olds and wondered - 'Why?'

Now I understand.

When your child is a toddler, you are thrilled everyone has made it through a year unscathed.

When they get to school age you realise just how quickly the time is going and you want to make memories which will never be forgotten.

And in reaching adulthood you appreciate you are there to celebrate with the ones you love full stop.

Too many do not have that chance.

*'Today you are You, that is truer than true.
There is no one alive who is Youer than You.'*
Dr. Suess

Birthday Parties by Claire Hainstock
Mum to Amy, Harry and Joe and company Acting the
Party. www.actingtheparty.co.uk

Fun, laughs, and delight weigh equally with organising,
stress, and cost. Parties are the stark reality of the
journey from being a child to becoming a parent. We
love to see our children having a good time so we lavish
almost a month's salary on plastic bits, terrible food
and entertainment so that we can invite two thirds of a
class that our child dislikes. What happened to the good
old days of party games and ice cream? Well, it ended
in tears and food fights. Party trends change, as adults,
however, we should realise we do have a choice.

*'Why is a birthday cake the only food you can
blow on and spit on and everybody rushes
to get a piece?'* Bobby Kelton

What Matters Most by Victoria Pearson
Victoria lives behind a keyboard, surrounded by the chaos
being married with three children, a dog and a very clumsy
cat creates. When she isn't running around screaming, "Be
careful" or picking up after someone she is generally to be
found writing stories. www.victoria-pearson.webs.com

I love Christmas, despite all of the stress leading up to it.
I love getting people gifts I know they'll love, and I hate

not knowing the right gift to give. I love the singing, the school plays, even inventing the nativity costumes (this year I did a sheep, a cow, and a snowman, but I have also made a partridge costume before) but nothing compares to the day itself. We spend the day all together, snuggled up and cosy.

Watching the children open their presents is amazing, but nothing compares to spending the day with the people you love.

> *'Life, love and laughter - what priceless*
> *gifts to give our children.'*
> *Phyllis Dryden*

We've Got a Surprise for you Mummy by Clare
Frazzled Mum to Finn (5yrs) and Nathaniel (3yrs), and wife to Jonathan, her unsung hero. Clare is also founder of www.nonslipbath.co.uk selling anti-slip bath safety stickers.

Three spilt drinks, two half eaten dinners, one you-need-to-make-a-sheep-costume- for-tomorrow letter from school and there really wasn't room for any more last straws. Then 'We've got a surprise for you Mummy'. I expected a scribbled picture of Yoda holding an ice cream. They explained that Mummy was going to a spa with her friends for the weekend. 'I think you should have a rest because when you are here we boss you around a bit too much,' said my sweet hearted 5 year old... and there was half an advent chocolate waiting for me when I got back. Now that's love.

'A rose can say "I love you"
Orchids can enthrall
But a weed bouquet in a chubby fist
yes, that says it all.'
Author Unknown

Not a Christmas Nativity by Charlie Plunkett
Mum to a gorgeous little boy called Cole and author of 'The True Diaries' series of books. www.charlieplunkett. co.uk

As a child I remember playing Mary in the Nativity and wondered what part my child would be given in his nursery Christmas show, would he be a shepherd? Tea-towels would make for a nice and easy costume. I'd never have guessed that his first appearance on stage would be as a lettuce! To be fair I excelled myself and made not just one lettuce costume but twenty, one for each child in his class.

This year my costume making skills are once again being put to the test as he is going to be a dolphin. Wish me luck!

'I know how to do anything - I'm a Mom.'
Roseanne Barr

Nativity Plays by Ruth-less Shanks
Mum to Ray, Arnie and Mini. Ruth started writing again when her Dad had a health scare and came to stay. Once he was better, he was kicked out (joke), but she carried on writing about trying to be a better daughter, sister, partner, mother, yada, yada in her blog. www.grand adcametotea.wordpress.com

Your child's first Nativity is a wonder. Yes, you stress they will lose their head-dress or wet themselves on stage, but through a blur of tears, you realise your whole life was leading to this moment. However, your seventh nativity is a bit...meh. Especially if, like mine, none of your children have once had an A-list role. "I'm gonna be a shepherd," Mini squeaks. "I'm a camel" Arnie boasts. Mini's mate runs past, "I'm Mary." Out the corner of your eye, you see Mary's proud mother. It takes all your Christmas spirit to not trip her over.

'I auditioned for the role of an angel in the Nativity play at school. I didn't get it. I auditioned for Mary; didn't get it. So I made up the character of the sheep who sat next to Baby Jesus.'
Nicole Kidman

A Conversation with my Grandson by Mary Dudley
Mum to three 'grown-up' daughters and grandma to eight wonderful grandchildren.

My grandson asks, 'What was Christmas like when you were young, did you have a lot of fun?'
'Yes I did. But back in 1953 we could not afford a Christmas tree, so mum and I collected twigs brought indoors and painted white, how wondrous they looked with fairy lights.
Chicken, mince-pies, pudding to eat and chocolate fingers, what a treat!
An annual of my favourite Rupert Bear and lots of ribbon for my hair.'
My grandson asks, 'What about computer games, DVDs?'
I say 'We never even had TV.'

'WHAT NO TV! That sort of Christmas is not for me!'

'My grandson was visiting one day when he asked,
"Gramma, do you know how you and God are
alike?" I mentally polished my halo while
I asked, "No, how are we alike?"
"You're both old," he replied.'
Author Unknown

The Tooth Fairy by Susan Spence
Mum of 4 Wife of 1, our lovely biggest boy has Asperger
Syndrome. www.mumof4wifeof1.blogspot.co.uk

My two eldest children are getting to the age where they are hearing rumours at school about the validity of the Tooth Fairy. For us it presents an additional problem.

My eldest son has Asperger Syndrome, so believes that everyone always tells the truth. I've recently had to answer the "Is the Tooth Fairy real?" question. I've deflected it for now, but I need to think of a good reason as to why I haven't told the truth thus far, and why he shouldn't pass the truth on to his younger siblings. And as for the big man in red...

'In spite of the six thousand manuals on child
raising in the bookstores, child raising is still
a dark continent and no one really knows
anything. You just need a lot of love and luck -
and, of course, courage.'
Bill Cosby

Why Did The Tooth Fairy Forget To Come Mummy? By Vanessa Wester
Mum of three lovely children, teacher, author and avid reader. www.vanessawesterwriter.blogspot.co.uk

My daughter lost her tooth whilst at school. A clever teacher made a cute envelope for the tooth, which my daughter diligently put under her pillow. The next morning my daughter woke up and brought the package in, all forlorn. "The Tooth Fairy forgot!"

I immediately said, "I'm sure she didn't. She must have liked the packaging so much she decided you should keep it. Let's put it out tonight, we can explain the tooth is inside."

Luckily, my daughter believed me and the Tooth Fairy 'came' the next day. You have to think on your toes as a parent.

'In this pocket you will find
A teensy, tiny tooth of mine.
So while I sleep where dreams are made,
Let's see if you can make a trade.'
Author Unknown

Learning

*'Do not train children to learning by force
and harshness, but direct them to it by what
amuses their minds, so that you may be
better able to discover with accuracy the
peculiar bent of the genius of each.'*
Plato

Loving a Baby by Deborah McNelis
Mother of Trisha and Tracy. Grandmother of Ava.
Deborah is owner of Brain Insights and author of 'The
Brain Development Series' www.braininsightsonline.com

There is a basic and vital need of all children.

Children have an essential need for love.

Love is best shown by responding to the expressed
needs of babies.

Babies express their needs through smiles, giggles and
cries.

Cries, giggles and smiles consistently responded to
helps babies' brains.

Brains of babies grow best when learning to trust.

Trust is developed through predictable loving care.

Care through loving interactions creates healthy
brain pathways.

Pathways in the brain are wired best when feeling loved.

Loved babies have brains ready for more learning.
Learning begins through the essential need babies
have for love.

> *'To those born into the gaze of loving eyes,*
> *life is beautiful. To those welcomed by*
> *tender voices, life is peaceful. To those*
> *embraced with gentle hands, life is secure.*
> *To those born into a world of compassion,*
> *life is good beyond all measure.'*
> *Anon*

The Benefits of Play by Claire Hainstock
Mum to Amy, Harry and Joe and company Acting the
Party. www.actingtheparty.co.uk

My child sits on the floor a toy in each hand, re-enacting
a fantasy in their head, their own special world.
Unaware that they are speaking out loud, podgy cheeks
puffing, relaxed and happy. With their friends this
takes on another form, testing, learning, demanding
and sub-serving. And as they get older the play is more
structured, desperate to put on shows to parents who,
although reluctant, do their best to feign interest. But
it should always be encouraged. Role-play sets us
apart, it is how we learn, listen and explore; by using our
imagination it will take us forward.

> *'Pausing to listen to an airplane in the sky,*
> *stooping to watch a ladybug on a plant, sitting on a*
> *rock to watch the waves crash over the quayside -*
> *children have their own agendas and timescales.*
> *As they find out more about their world and*

their place in it, they work hard not to let adults
hurry them. We need to hear their voices.'
Cathy Nutbrown

Let's Pretend by Sarah
Proud mum of two adopted boys. Lover of crafts, cooking
and all things vintage www.thepuffindiaries.wordpress.com

As my two adopted children came from a background
of neglect it was explained to us that their imaginative
play would be limited. Too much stress and anxiety to
stop relax, imagine and play. Over the years we have
enjoyed sitting with them, acting out scenarios and
watching them tentatively join in. The phrase "let's
pretend", at first spoken with hesitation and uncertainty
for the unknown world they may deliver, now trips of
the tongue and is woven into every game. Sometimes as
I sit on the stairs listening to their world of "let's pretend"
I know we've come far.

'Children need the freedom and time to play.
Play is not a luxury. Play is a necessity.'
Kay Redfield Jamison

Preparing Children For Life: Learning Key Life Skills by
Dr Rosina McAlpine
An award-winning educator turning the science of
child development into the art of parenting. Founder of
'Inspired Children: life skills for kids in just 15 minutes
at a time' www.inspiredchildren.com

I have taught university students for over 25 years now
and their biggest stumbling block is their lack of key life

skills. To succeed in the world children need to feel good about themselves, be able to interact effectively with others and resolve conflicts, manage their finances and their time as well as take care of their health by eating properly, resting and exercising. Parents often focus on supporting a child's academic achievement, but this is not enough to help children navigate this world successfully. Help your children develop key life skills and they'll have skills for a great life.

> *'The child is like a foreigner who doesn't know*
> *the language, isn't familiar with the street plan,*
> *is ignorant of the laws and customs of the land.*
> *At times, he likes to go exploring on his own;*
> *when things get rough he asks for directions*
> *and help. What he needs is a guide who*
> *will politely answer his questions.'*
> *Janusz Korczak*

Things My Parents Taught Me by Charlie Plunkett
Mum to a gorgeous little boy called Cole and author of 'The True Diaries' series of books. www.charlieplunkett.co.uk

To cook, sew and do D.I.Y. They encouraged me to be creative and enjoy the big outdoors. They inspired me by example and showed me that anything is possible if you put your mind to it. They trusted me to make my own decisions and never preached to me about my mistakes. They made me feel capable and beautiful; they gave me wings to explore the world. They are always there for me at the end of the phone. Everything that I am I owe to my parents and all this I hope to pass on to my beloved son.

'Don't worry that children never listen to you;
worry that they are always watching you.'
Robert Fulghum

Love Maths? By Stephanie Cracknell
Founder of Mathemagical, making maths fun for pre-school children, winner of the 'Woman in Education' award and mum of two lovely children. www.mathemagical.co.uk

Parents often say to me in absolute surprise "My toddler really loves maths, he already counts to 25!"
But …
Colouring teaches shape.
Splashing water teaches volume.
Sand is mass and weight.
Count the blocks in the playroom.
The empty loo roll is a cylinder.
The hairclips need sorting.
All the different sized teddies.
Always need ordering.
Money in the sweet shop.
Division: that's yours, this mine.
One more biscuit is addition.
Mr Wolf tells the time.
So why do kids love maths?
Cos when all is said and done It's everywhere they look and play.
Maths is fun!

'There are no seven wonders of the world
in the eyes of a child. There are seven million.'
Walt Streightiff

On Writing by Ruth-less Shanks
Mum to Ray, Arnie and Mini. Ruth started writing again when her Dad had a health scare and came to stay. Once he was better, he was kicked out (joke), but she carried on writing about trying to be a better daughter, sister, partner, mother, yada, yada in her blog. www.grand adcametotea.wordpress.com

Mini scrawls M's across pages and trails them around the house. Dragons teeth, they look like mountain ranges. Strong and in control like her. Husband makes impressed faces at me. But Arnie, 16 months older, can't write yet. He is left-handed too. It's odd to have a left-hander in the family - a little cuckoo in our nest. Grandad, old school, told him to use his right hand. It made Arnie cry. I explained, "Hey, it's ok..." We don't understand the genetics but I remember he came out of me, one arm aloft, like Superman. Perhaps that did it.

> *'While we try to teach our children all about life,*
> *our children teach us what life is all about.'*
> *Angela Schwindt*

Grow a Musician by Jenny Worstall
Author, teacher and mother. www.jennyworstall.webspace. virginmedia.com

Enjoy an early musical start with your child.
Sing to your baby (Yes, you can!), listen to music with them on your knee, dance with them, talk about music (that sounds like some monkeys jumping...), take them to concerts and play an instrument to them (dust down your old school recorder).

Leave instruments around at home - the piano should be open, the keyboard plugged in, the kazoo within reach.

Start formal lessons when they're ready. Strings are ideal as they come in tiny sizes.

Help them practise, sit and listen to them perform and always praise them.

Have fun!

> *'Music washes away from the soul the*
> *dust of everyday life.'*
> Berthold Auerbach

A Perfect Children's Yoga Practise by Sarah Cooper
Yogini mum of 3 and specialist prenatal, postnatal and baby yoga teacher and founder of the company Sarah's Baby Yoga. www.sarahsbabyyoga.co.uk

Be under no illusions that yoga with my children is a calm and peaceful affair, despite me being a yoga teacher!

A Classic Example:

Warm-up - Led by one of my older children (and slightly random!)

Sun Salutations - Punctuated by my youngest, diving under anything looking remotely like an archway (dog poses/lunges), while we cheer him on with "Quick the doors are closing!" Handstands - By all with applause for everyone (regardless of any support needed!) Relaxation - In a heap of giggles while we lie together and chatter about anything and everything! Its chaos! And it's perfect!

'A teacher's job is to take a bunch of live wires
and see that they are well-grounded.'
D. Martin

The Importance of Pastimes by Diane Mannion
Freelance copywriter at: www.dianemannion.co.uk
and author of 'Kids' Clubs and Organizations' available
from Amazon.

Pastimes can teach children practical skills that aren't
always taught at school. There are thousands of kids'
clubs in the UK covering a wide range of pastimes from
sports to animal care to volunteering. These clubs enable
children to have fun and interact with others that have
similar interests. Non-academic children can discover
talents outside the classroom, which helps to improve
self-esteem. Additionally, for older children there is the
chance to gain useful qualifications that can help
with future career opportunities. Surprisingly a lot of
children's clubs and groups are inexpensive so it's well
worth exploring what is on offer.

'Children's games are hardly games. Children
are never more serious than when they play.'
Montaigne, Essays.

School and University

'One looks back with appreciation to the brilliant teachers, but with gratitude to those who touched our human feelings. The curriculum is so much necessary raw material, but warmth is the vital element for the growing plant and for the soul of the child.'
Carl Jung

Getting Ready for School by Charlie Plunkett
Mum to a gorgeous little boy called Cole and author of 'The True Diaries' series of books. www.charlieplunkett. co.uk

Helping your child to be confident at using the toilet is a must as well as washing their hands. Make a game of practising putting clothes and shoes on and off. Take a visit to the school beforehand and read books about starting school. Try to get in a routine of going to bed and getting up at the same time each day. Encourage your child to write their name and involve them in the purchase of school uniform. If they have friends going to the same school have a play date beforehand and most importantly enjoy this latest milestone!

'I wish I could remember my name. Mummy said it would come in useful. Like wellies. When there's

puddles. Yellow wellies. I wish she was here.
I think my name is sewn on somewhere. Perhaps
the teacher will read it for me. Tea-cher. The one
who makes the tea.' Extract from 'First day
at School' by Roger McGough

Preparing for School by Joanne Phillips
Author and mother to Lulu aged 4. www.joannephillips.
co.uk

I wasn't a wreck the first day my daughter started school,
it was the days leading up to it that floored me. I confess,
a part of me had always secretly looked forward to the
school years. They represented a certain freedom for me
and a new stage of life for her. But then the wobbles
started. I felt threatened, disconnected, confused. It was
too soon; she was too young. How would she cope?
How would I? It also represented the passing of time; as
she gets older, I get older. Of course, she was fine. And
so was I.

'The mother-child relationship is paradoxical and,
in a sense, tragic. It requires the most intense love
on the mother's side, yet this very love must
help the child grow away from the mother,
and to become fully independent.'
Erich Fromm

First Day at School by Pippa
Mum to Laila (5yrs) and Cameron (2 ½ yrs)

If you want to join the majority of parents on this day
then take a travel size pack of tissues and blub in the

playground. This however wasn't me. I felt immense pride and happiness, not sadness, that my little girl was so eager to start at school and essentially on a new adventure in her life, one which for the first time didn't involve her parents. In my mind I'm preparing my children to be independent beings not tied to my apron strings and I'll leave my sobbing for the day this is truly accomplished and they leave home.

'A mother is not a person to lean on,
but a person to make leaning unnecessary.'
Dorothy Canfield Fisher

Overcoming It All To Go To School by Victoria Pearson
Victoria lives behind a keyboard, surrounded by the chaos being married with three children, a dog and a very clumsy cat creates. When she isn't running around screaming, "Be careful" or picking up after someone she is generally to be found writing stories. www.victoria-pearson.webs.com

My youngest was born needing several bouts of open heart surgery, the first at nine days and the second at seven months after going into heart failure. We had been told during our pregnancy that getting through his first year was going to be his biggest challenge, and boy were the surgeons right! He had so much to deal with.

On his first school day he was unrecognisable as that panting, weak little blue baby.

He walked in with his peers, indistinguishable from them, as strong and tall. I thought I would burst with pride at my little miracle boy.

'Thorns and stings
And those such things
Just make stronger
Our angel wings.'
Terri Guillemets

Empty Buggy Syndrome by Charlie Plunkett
Mum to a gorgeous little boy called Cole and author of
'The True Diaries' series of books. www.charlieplunkett.
co.uk

I can't believe that the "Big Day" came so quickly. One
minute Cole was a babe in arms and the next he was
ready for school!

The three of us walked to "big school". We were
greeted by his teacher, placed his belongings on a peg,
water container and banana were present and correct.
The tambourine sounded, signalling time for parents to
leave. Cole ran to sit with the other children on the
carpet with hardly a backward glance. We blew him a
kiss and pushed an empty buggy home feeling a little sad
but proud of our gorgeous boy.

'Learning is a treasure that will
follow its owner everywhere.'
Chinese Proverb

Home from School by Ruth-less Shanks
Mum to Ray, Arnie and Mini. Ruth started writing again
when her Dad had a health scare and came to stay. Once
he was better, he was kicked out (joke), but she carried
on writing about trying to be a better daughter, sister,

161

partner, mother, yada, yada in her blog. www.grand adcametotea.wordpress.com

Arnie can't believe school is five days and the weekend is only two. I agree it's unfair.

The children queue at the reception gate and wait to be claimed. In their uniforms, the kids look the same. My arm is in a semi-permanent wave until Arnie shyly appears.

"What did you do today?" I ask after he pees up the nearest tree.

"Nothing!"

Yesterday, he told me he had an apple at break.

We pick up my Dad.

"I've been calling all day. Where were you?"

"Nowhere," I sigh.

Grandad looks at me like I look at Arnie. Really?

*'I have never let my schooling
interfere with my education.'*
Mark Twain

A French Education Part One by Bev Spicer
Qualified teacher and lecturer in EFL, specialising in Phonetics and Pronunciation. Bev has been a legal secretary, Sunday checkout girl and Playboy croupier. Currently writing books in SW France, living in a Charentaise house with a renovation-mad husband and two enormous teenage boys. www.baspicer. blogspot.fr

I sent my boys (then 9 and 12) to school in France the day after we arrived. The headmaster assured me, in

French, that they'd be fine. Their teachers told me, in French, that they'd soon get the hang of it. Harry and Alfie learned poems in French and brought home French books to read about Sinbad, and extracts from Homer's The Odyssey. They liked school lunches and the half-day on Wednesdays, but not the 8 o'clock starts or the ban on football in the playground. Alfie received an early warning for flicking a mushroom onto a dinner lady's shoe!

'The larger the island of knowledge,
the longer the shoreline of wonder.'
Ralph W. Sockman

A Hug a Day by Ellie
Busy mum of two and author of 'The Mummy Diary'.
www.themummydiary.co.uk

This morning as my son's friends arrived in the playground, they all gave each other a hug. This was something I'd observed when he was at nursery; it was lovely to see that even though they are at school, they are still young enough to want to do this. It is true to say my heart melted and for that moment the world seemed so innocent. If only when I turned up to work someone would give me a hug, I think the world would be a nicer place. Because a hug is a great way to start the day.

'The most precious jewels you'll ever have
around your neck are...the arms
of your children.'
Anon

School Bug by Charlie Plunkett
Mum to a gorgeous little boy called Cole and author of 'The True Diaries' series of books. www.charlieplunkett. co.uk

It was inevitable that the combination of a classroom of thirty children all coughing and spluttering would result in something unpleasant.

12 pm I'm woken by Cole crying, as I lift him from his bed he is sick everywhere. I clean him up, calm him down and pop him back to bed. Half an hour later and we repeat this, only I'm not quick enough getting him to the bathroom and he vomits down my back. On and off this continues all night. By 9 am we have an enormous pile of laundry, one poorly boy and an exhausted mummy!

> *'Mother - that was the bank where we deposited all our hurts and worries.'*
> T. DeWitt Talmage

PE Kit by Sarah Gorrell
BBC Sussex and Surrey Drivetime presenter and mum of four.

An early childhood memory: rummaging through the "spare" PE kit amongst an array of unsightly, smelly articles. Then the humiliation of sporting activities in oversized, flapping shorts. At moments like this you vow to be the sort of parent who never forgets to send their child to School neatly ironed and organised. Recently my six year old came home with a note "Dear Mummy and Daddy, please remember my PE kit." Horrible maternal guilt followed. Visions of my child penning her solitary reminder while everyone else joyfully cavorted, engaged in sporting activities. Makes you more forgiving of your own parents!

'If you promise not to believe everything
your child says happens at school,
I'll promise not to believe everything
he says happens at home.'
Anonymous Teacher

First Impressions Count by Sarah Wood
Mum of three and blogger www.mumofthreeworld. blogspot.com

As my boy set off for his new school in his new blazer he looked so smart and handsome and grown up. I wondered what impression he would make. Because first impressions count and they start on day one. I bought him a cool school bag. Superdry. It's not just that I want the cool kids to like him, it's that I don't want anyone to actively DISLIKE him. Because having someone actively dislike you at secondary school is not easy. So with his own beautiful face and his cool school bag, I am setting him on the right path.

'Nothing you do for a child is ever wasted.'
Garrison Keillor

A French Education Part Two by Bev Spicer
Mum and author of 'Bunny on a Bike', 'My Grandfather's Eyes', 'A Good Day to Jump' and 'Angels'. www.baspicer.blogspot.fr

Four years on and my sons could speak fluent French. They learnt more in one term than they had in a school year in England, in terms of factual information, although learning by rote for weekly tests may not be the only way to go, in my opinion.

'England or France?' I asked them recently. I expected them to say 'England!' as they always had done before, usually followed by, 'Why did you force us to come here?' But they looked at each other and agreed that they really couldn't decide between the two. 'How about Spain, then?' I suggested.

> *'The whole purpose of education is to
> turn mirrors into windows.'*
> Sydney J. Harris

Starting Secondary School by Suzanne Whitton
Mum to three gorgeous children and 1 crazy pooch. You can find her blogging about parenting at her website. www.3childrenandit.blogspot.co.uk

Nothing can prepare you for the moment your child starts secondary school.

As she proudly tries on the new, grown-up uniform, the child you have nurtured, protected and guided through primary school suddenly looks different. Different from the outside, yet still the same vulnerable child that you so desperately want to cocoon into a shell of protection, on the inside. Trying so very hard not to convey any sign of fear or apprehension, you wave her off with a cheery 'goodbye' as she embarks on a new journey - another step away from you and one step nearer to adulthood.

'Being a role model is the most powerful form of educating. Youngsters need good role models more than they need critics. It's one of parents greatest responsibilities and opportunities.'
John Wooden

The Letter is the Law by Sarah Wood
Mum of three and blogger www.mumofthreeworld. blogspot.com

At primary school, The letter is the law. If it isn't in a letter, it isn't sufficiently important for me to worry about forgetting something, being somewhere, paying for something, wearing something, making something or taking something in. At secondary school, it's a different ball game. My son played violin in his first school concert the other day. It was a prestigious occasion. We had a letter about the tickets. We had a letter about the rehearsal at the Town Hall. We DIDN'T have a letter about when he needed to be back at the Town Hall in the evening.

'Home computers are being called upon to perform many new functions, including the consumption of homework formerly eaten by the dog.'
Doug Larson

Saying Goodbye. For Now...by Mark Richards
Mark started writing a weekly column about his children ten years ago. He's gone from nativity plays and party bags to teenage angst, slamming doors and boyfriends he's - wisely - not told about. You can find his 'Best Dad I Can Be' books on the Kindle and follow the battle with his teenage children. www.bestdadicanbe.com

Son or daughter starting university soon? Here's a simple quiz…

Everything's unpacked. It's time to go. As you bid your child a tearful farewell do they say? a) Thanks for all your love and support over the last 18 years, Mum and Dad. I couldn't have got here without you. b) Have a safe trip home and I'll send you a 500 word e-mail twice a week with all my news. c) What? Are you still here?

Think the answer is one of the first two options? Your children must be under five. Or you need to increase your medication.

'Helping your eldest to pick a college is one of the greatest educational experiences of life - for the parents. Next to trying to pick his bride, it's the best way to learn that your authority, if not entirely gone, is slipping fast.'
Sally and James Reston

The Joyful Reunion by Mark Richards
Mark started writing a weekly column about his children ten years ago. He's gone from nativity plays and party bags to teenage angst, slamming doors and boyfriends he's - wisely - not told about. You can find his 'Best Dad I Can Be' books on the Kindle and follow the battle with his teenage children. www.bestdadicanbe.com

And then we collected him…

We were about to see our son. The one we hadn't seen for more than two months.

Our first child. The baby I held in my arms 19 years ago.

Nervous? Yes, I think we were.

Would Tom have missed us? Would he shed a tear? Would our son have changed?

What would his first words be?

"Good grief, Dad. What's that on your face?"

"It's Movember, son. Thought I'd leave it on. Let you see it. Pretty cool, eh?"

"Shave it off, Dad. You look like someone who's been kidnapped and held for ransom."

'There is nothing wrong with today's teenager that twenty years won't cure. 'Author Unknown

Teenagers

'Adolescence is a period of rapid changes.
Between the ages of 12 and 17, for example,
a parent ages as much as 20 years.'
Author Unknown

They're Really Butterflies... by Teresa Hamilton
An author, online store owner and mum to three children who are swiftly flying the nest. If life with toddlers was hectic it's nothing to life with teenagers...but she wouldn't trade it for the world. She can be found at www.teresahamilton.co.uk writing about life as she knows it.

If it's too far back for you to remember what it was like to be a teenager I will remind you. It is hard. Teenagers are caterpillars trapped in their cocoons, struggling to work out which butterfly they want to be. Yes, they sleep a lot, are self-obsessed and don't appreciate all the things you do for them but guaranteed, they will emerge one day.

Don't be fooled by their adult sized appearance, they are children underneath that need boundaries and your support. Ask yourself before you explode next time, does it really matter? Pick which battles to fight carefully.

*'Adolescents are not monsters. They are just
people trying to learn how to make it among
the adults in the world, who are probably
not so sure themselves.'*
Virginia Satir

Surviving Teenagers by The 40 Year Old Domestic Goddess
Exhausted mother to 'The Teenager' and also 'The Whirlwind'. www.40yearolddomesticgoddess. blogspot.com

Raising a Teenager is as frustrating as nailing jelly to a tree. Here are my top tips to surviving the first few years.

Never make eye contact during an argument, this only makes them crosser.

Always nod and smile at them, they cannot lie whilst you are doing this.

Do not bother with Google, Teenagers know everything.

Record this message onto a disc, "Hurry up, clean your teeth, you're late" this will save you repeating it 100 times. Start playing this message at 8 am.

Learn the art of grunting, this will be your only form of communication for 5 years.

*'Telling a teenager the facts of life is
like giving a fish a bath.'*
Arnold H. Glasow

Mothers of Teenagers by Annabel, Grace and Ellie
Edited excerpt from Parenting Pitfalls section of The CountryWives' Blog www.countrywives.co.uk/category/ parenting-pitfalls

Teenagers often seem so selfish - mobile phones have exacerbated this by allowing kids to constantly re-organise their arrangements. For parents this means that one minute you have six kids eating supper and staying the night, the next fourteen, and finally only three pitch up and then bugger off for a pizza and sleep at someone else's house. Best decision recently was not to let their comings and goings get us hot under the collar. It's paid dividends - they are much less tricky now that we're so amenable, we are less stressed because we only buy food that can be refrozen!

> *'Teenagers complain there's nothing to do,*
> *then stay out all night doing it.'*
> Bob Phillips

Bedrooms and Clutter by Teresa Hamilton
An author, online store owner and mum to three children who are swiftly flying the nest. If life with toddlers was hectic it's nothing to life with teenagers...but she wouldn't trade it for the world. She can be found at www.teresahamilton.co.uk writing about life as she knows it.

If the sight of your teenager's bedroom gets you heated, plan your campaign. Ask yourself: have you ever shown them how to organize their environment, or just always done it for them? If the answer is that they are just plain lazy, you have one of two options to remain sane because more nagging will fall on deaf ears. Either collect up the clutter into black sacks and hide in a corner so you don't have to look at it or always keep the door shut. There will come a time for negotiation when they run out of clean underwear.

'There isn't a child who hasn't gone out into the brave new world who eventually doesn't return to the old homestead carrying a bundle of dirty clothes.'
Art Buchwald

The Differences Between Girls and Boys by The 40 Year Old Domestic Goddess.
Exhausted mother to 'The Teenager' and 'The Whirlwind'.
www.40yearolddomesticgoddess.blogspot.com

Teenagers. Spot The Difference.

Girls
Take about a day to get ready and fill the whole house with various nice smells.
Boys
Take 2 seconds to get ready and choke the whole house with various revolting smells.
Girls
Spend ages getting their school bags ready making sure all homework is in plastic folders.
Boys
Spend as little time as possible getting their carrier bag ready making sure homework is screwed up to the best of their ability.
Girls
Will wear things once.
Boys
Will find ways to wear things more than once even if it means turning them inside out.

'It's difficult to decide whether growing pains are something teenagers have - or are.'
Author Unknown

Fashion Sense by Mark Richards
Mark started writing a weekly column about his children ten years ago. He's gone from nativity plays and party bags to teenage angst, slamming doors and boyfriends he's - wisely - not told about. You can find his 'Best Dad I Can Be' books on the Kindle and follow the battle with his teenage children. www.bestdadicanbe.com

As a parent there are certain rites of passage: the first day at school; the first time your child rolls home drunk. For a Dad, the first time your teenage daughter gives you fashion advice is another. She was 13. She'd conned me into a trip to Next. But maybe there was just enough space on my credit card for a new shirt.

"What do you think of this, darling?" I said, holding up a particularly fine green and purple striped number. She looked at me coldly. "Daddy," she said. "There are dead people with more fashion sense than you."

> *'Violet will be a good color for hair at just*
> *about the same time that brunette*
> *becomes a good color for flowers.'*
> *Fran Lebowitz*

Muddy Waters! by Richard Denman
This is about me and my 16 year old son at the end of our break in Dorset with me sending him home muddy to his mum! Author of the poetry book 'Love Life' (available from Amazon).

Us 'boys' waiting our turn on a
mid-summers day soggy and wet!

Just perfect for quad biking!
Don't fret,
this is England!
Raincoats on, helmets on,
away we go!
Along a muddy track to a
steep bend
that looks like a ditch,
full of mud and ...
no, not that! So much
water more like a pond
then a pool, adrenaline
pumping I drive straight through.
A torrent of muddy water hits me
full force!
Such a farce that it makes
us laugh.
An hour of mud, jumps and
bumps.
A shame to be done after so much fun!

'Childhood is that wonderful time of life
when all you need to do to lose
weight is take a bath.'
Author Unknown

A Sense of Humour by Teresa Hamilton
An author, online store owner and mum to three children who are swiftly flying the nest. If life with toddlers was hectic it's nothing to life with teenagers... but she wouldn't trade it for the world. She can be found at www.teresahamilton.co.uk writing about life as she knows it.

As with all dealings with teenagers, a sense of humour is a bonus. Yes, they think you know nothing, are excruciatingly embarrassing and have no idea what they are going through but if you can find a connection to keep communicating there aren't any subjects that are taboo. Never dismiss their ideas, they will eventually stop telling you them and you could miss out on so much. Rather be chilled, find an activity you can share together. They may have more knowledge of a subject than you they can share - you never know; you may grow to like dubstep music?

'You can tell a child is growing up when he stops asking where he came from and starts refusing to tell where he is going.'
Author Unknown

Hug Them Anyway... By Jennifer M. Hatfield M.H.S, ccc/slp.
Jennifer is a Mom to two children, business owner and speech language pathologist. She is currently navigating her way through a tween in middle school and teen preparing to leave the nest. You can find her (and her blog) at www.therapyandlearning services.com

Teenagers are grouchy...hug them anyway.
Teenagers are smelly...hug them anyway.
Teenagers are INFURIATING...hug them anyway.
Teenagers are know it alls...hug them anyway.
Teenagers are irresponsible...hug them anyway.
Teenagers are stubborn...hug them anyway.

Hugs turn teenagers into... Hopeful dreamers, enthusiastic livers, caring humans, friends, happy helpers and balanced adults.

Hugs communicate love, hope, SAFETY, do-overs, forgiveness and HOME.

Teens won't remember much of what we say...but they will remember what we DID.

Hug them anyway...even when their arms are plastered to their sides and you hear utter disgust emanate from their compressed lips.

'Sometimes it's better to put love into
hugs than to put it into words.'
Author Unknown

The N Word by Teresa Hamilton
An author, online store owner and mum to three children who are swiftly flying the nest. If life with toddlers was hectic it's nothing to life with teenagers...but she wouldn't trade it for the world. She can be found at www.teresahamilton.co.uk writing about life as she knows it.

The worst word you can utter to a teenager is 'No!' Remember these are toddlers disguised as adults, the N word is guaranteed to bring on a tantrum. Instead always start with a 'maybe', 'possibly' or 'let's talk about it'. That gives you a chance to open negotiations instead of just staring as the teenager storms off. You could discuss the practical reasons why getting home so late at night or having a Facebook party isn't such a good idea. 'I'm not trying to stop you having fun, just trying to keep you safe,' is a good way to start.

*'I tell my child, if I seem obsessed to always
know where you've been, it is because my
DNA will be found at the scene.'*
Robert Brault

Engaging with Teenagers by Diane Mannion
Freelance copywriter at: www.dianemannion.co.uk
and author of 'Kids' Clubs and Organizations' available
from Amazon.

As children grow into teenagers they often prefer their
own space so it is important to find ways to continue
communicating. Try asking them about their day even if
you don't always get much response. To allow natural
conversation to take place, eat meals together around the
dining table. You could also try eating out as a family.

Weekly family meetings are another good idea. Calmly
air your grievances but also praise them for anything they
have done well. Allow them to present their views then
agree a sensible way forward. This can help to maintain
harmony in the home.

*'It's the three pairs of eyes that mothers have to
have...One pair that see through closed doors.
Another in the back of her head...and, of course,
the ones in front that can look at a child when
he goofs up and reflect 'I understand and I love
you' without so much as uttering a word.'*
Erma Bombeck

Think Positive by Teresa Hamilton
An author, online store owner and mum to three children
who are swiftly flying the nest. If life with toddlers was

hectic it's nothing to life with teenagers...but she wouldn't trade it for the world. She can be found at www. teresahamilton.co.uk writing about life as she knows it.

Life with a teenager can be such fun. Life with more than one is a bonus. If you can let the positives outweigh the negatives they will keep you in tune with the latest gadgets, music, fashion and TV programs, to name just a few things. Okay, so you won't like everything but isn't it worth having your own personal guide to show you what's out there? In turn you can continue to nurture them along life's road with the same unconditional love and care that you took when they were babies. Best of all they will keep you young.

*'The troubles of adolescence eventually all go away -
it's just like a really long, bad cold.'*
Dawn Ruelas

The Night You've Been Dreading by Mark Richards
Mark started writing a weekly column about his children ten years ago. He's gone from nativity plays and party bags to teenage angst, slamming doors and boyfriends he's - wisely - not told about. You can find his 'Best Dad I Can Be' books on the Kindle and follow the battle with his teenage children. www.bestdadicanbe.com

Finally, the night you've dreaded. Your son phones...
    "I'm really, drunk. I'm coming up the hill. Can you get me?"
    Well, it had to happen sooner or later. I pulled some jeans on and yelled to my wife.
    "Jane, quick, we're going out."

"What are you talking about?"

"It's Tom. He's drunk."

"What do mean drunk?"

"I mean he's completely paralytic and we need to go for him. Not in my car though."

No way was I risking Tom throwing up in my car. I set off jogging down the road.

Thirty seconds later Jane passed me. In my car.

> *'Small children disturb your sleep,*
> *big children your life.'*
> *Yiddish Proverb*

All in a Swirl (My eldest on the trip of a lifetime) by Richard Denman

Dad of two now grown up young people who are also like best friends. He tries hard not to stumble over himself which is quite a task. Richard is author of the poetry book 'Love Life' (available from Amazon).

> Here you are about to fly high
> yet it seems so soon.
> I remember so vividly that baby
> that would sometimes cry,
> though not often, as you were
> a happy child.
> But here we are;
> you, your nanny, best friend Nel:
> a special group for a special day,
> all because you're flying to Aus.
> Emotions swell as we ready
> to bid you farewell.
> A last drink at the bar then it's

Time.
I choke, I stutter, heart in a flutter.
Final words we utter.
Then you're gone in a flash,
a swirl as you throw a wave
and a twirl.

'Life is either a great adventure or nothing.'
Helen Keller

Grandparents

*'Nobody can do for little children what
grandparents do. Grandparents sort of sprinkle
stardust over the lives of little children.'*
Alex Haley

On Becoming a Grandparent by Dilys Morgan
Journalist, counsellor, blogger and broadcaster. Having
raised two sons and a daughter to adulthood is now
the very proud grandmother of two delightful boys and
founder of www.grandparentsnow.com

Becoming a Grandparent usually involves a jumble of
feelings: we may not feel ready yet, but we feel intensely
curious to meet this new human being. Once the
grandchild arrives, most of us are simply overwhelmed
by one single emotion - that of simple, unadulterated,
unconditional love.

And as the child grows, learns to recognise faces, smiles
and responds, a whole new world of mutual love is
unlocked. What makes this so special is that it's unexpected:
we never knew there were more opportunities for love in
our lives and it turns out to be a great bonus of later life.

'A garden of Love grows in a Grandmother's heart.'
Author Unknown

Grandchildren by Eileen Stuart
Mum to 3 wonderful children and Grandma to 2 gorgeous little boys who mean the world to her. Never fear being a Grandparent, it's the best thing imaginable.
www.thesearegrandmasthoughts.wordpress.com

They turn your world upside down.
They wrap you around their little fingers.
They play you off against their parents.
They make you smile, laugh, and cry.
They make you do things you haven't done for years.
They bring even MORE sleepless nights.
They bring chaos to your newly ordered home.
They get way with things your children never did.
They cause more fears and anxieties.
They miss you for all the right reasons.
They tell you secrets they never should.
They offer hugs just when you need them.
They bring you joy and happiness.
They steal your heart away.

> *'A grandmother is a little bit parent, a little bit teacher, and a little bit best friend.'*
> *Author Unknown*

Definition of a Grandparent by Mary Dudley
Mum to three 'grown-up' daughters and grandma to eight wonderful grandchildren.

What is the definition of a grandparent?
    Someone who may be on the slope, but definitely not over the hill.

Grandparents have infinite wisdom with life experiences behind them.

They provide stability, mediating skills between sometimes misunderstood grandchild and parent. Having inherited your genes you bond with grandchildren, sometimes seeing yourself in them.

In law they count for nothing, but grandparents love their grandchild as they did their own.

Having a grandchild gives you the will to focus to the future to evolve with them.

But most of all their love and humour are boundless and never fail to amaze.

> *'Grandmother-grandchild relationships*
> *are simple. Grandmas are short on*
> *criticism and long on love.'*
> Author Unknown

The Do's of Grandparenting by Dilys Morgan
Journalist, counsellor, blogger and broadcaster. Having raised two sons and a daughter to adulthood is now the very proud grandmother of two delightful boys and founder of www.grandparentsnow.com

DO dote on them; child-proof your home - put valuables/poisons up high and use locks and gates with abandon; spread plastic under high-chairs to catch drips and drops; buy toys/presents at Charity Shops; keep a plentiful supply of plasters; wear clothes with pockets filled with healthy snacks and wipes; abide by parents' rules and boundaries; always tell parents when they've been good - and give them credit; go to bed early when they stay over; keep certain activities 'special' for them;

prepare meals in advance; smother them with love; spoil them; take lots of photos and videos.

'No cowboy was ever faster on the draw
than a grandparent pulling a baby
picture out of a wallet.'
Anon

All The Stars In The Sky by Wendy Reynolds
Writer, Director, Choreographer and Scenic Artist and most of all, a proud Mum to 4 fantastic children, 1 girl and 3 boys. Nanny to 3 younger grandchildren, Nan to 4 older grandchildren and Nanna to 2 great grandchildren and each are adorable and amazing in their own way. My parting shot when I leave is 'I love you all the stars in the sky'.

'I'm passionately in love'
That's all I can say.
Caught in a web of wonder
Of blessings night and day.
My children were a wondrous joy
As each one came along,
Now my children's children
Breathe happiness and song.
I love their little faces
Their hands as they take mine
I love their cries for Nanny
As I say goodbye.
I am a Nan, a Nanny,
Unorthodox it's said,
I join my Grandchildren
As they jump upon my bed.

Love, joy and passion,
I sit and smile and sigh
I love my little darlings
'All the stars in the sky'.

*'Grandmas hold our tiny hands for just
a little while, but our hearts forever.'*
Author Unknown

The Difference Between Parenting and Grandparenting
by Brian V. Menard
Author and Computer Systems Engineer. Brian is the author of Learning How To Eat (Again) www.thebest dietbook.com and The Test Slayers Handbook www. thetestslayer.wordpress.com

Grandparents are lucky!

We get to express all the love we had for our own children but were not allowed to show them. It would be impossible to raise children properly if they knew how great our love was for them. Grandparents never need to discipline their grandkids or set boundaries on proper nutrition, regulate the time they come home or tell them how to dress. We can be a loving "true friend".

As a new parent, I recall my mother saying "If I had known how much fun my grandkids would be, I would have preferred having them instead."

*'To become a grandparent is to enjoy one
of the few pleasures in life for which the
consequences have already been paid.'*
Robert Brault

A Two Year Old Granddaughter's Favourite Game with her Doting Granddad by Roger Darlington
Roger is a 64 year old portfolio worker and blogger.
www.rogerdarlington.me.uk/nighthawk

Catrin's best fun with me is a climbing game. I sit down with her standing on my lap and holding her hands up in the air. She climbs up my chest and onto my shoulders, standing high and proud, but still holding on to my hands. We then pretend that she falls, but I'm still holding her hands and 'catch' her with my outstretched legs. She shrieks with excitement and the game ends when I release her hands and tickle her chin while she laughs hysterically. When I fall back smiling broadly, she looks up at me and cries: "Again!"

> *'Grandchildren don't stay young forever,*
> *which is good because Pop-pops have only*
> *so many horsey rides in them.'*
> *Gene Perret*

Being a Granddad by Anthony Fernau
Proud father of three amazing grown-up children, and adoring Grandpa of Toby. 'My wife and family are the most important part of my life.'

I like being a Granddad. I adore my four year old Grandson, Toby. He's definitely a 'boy-shaped-boy'. His mum calls him 'Pickle'. And he is. Full of beans, bags of energy, and talks very well for his age. Oh yes, and he is mad about trains. Just like I am, so perhaps he gets that from Grandpa, as he calls me. Toby lives in Canada but has flown more air miles in four years than I have in my entire life. When he's older perhaps he will come on his own to see his Grandpa. I'd like that.

'A grandfather is someone with silver in his hair and gold in his heart.'
Author Unknown

The Don'ts of Grandparenting by Dilys Morgan
Journalist, counsellor, blogger and broadcaster. Having raised two sons and a daughter to adulthood is now the very proud grandmother of two delightful boys and founder of www.grandparentsnow.com

Don't criticise their parents' methods of child-rearing; buy your grandchildren expensive outfits which you'll never see them wear; worry if they don't eat their vegetables when with you; buy safety equipment or car seats second-hand; let them get away with murder or emotional blackmail; listen to 'Mummy lets us' without checking first; expect to get a good night's sleep; worry about looking a mess - they won't mind!; care what other people think when you're out and about; fit cream carpet; give them felt tip pens and leave the room; let them out of sight; lose them.

'Grandmother - a wonderful mother with lots of practice.'
Author Unknown

Visitors from the Other Side of the World by Keith Pockett
Father to Beccy, Gemma and Jo and Grandfather to six, including Sophie (5) and Tom (3)

It had been nine long months and they had grown. They were excited and so were we. We love them both and they love us, no questions, unconditional, wonderful.

We live by a river, my river where I grew up. The train runs alongside; a steaming, fire eating train with a smell that defines the word "nostalgia". I happily re-live my boyhood vicariously through them.

"Will you hold my hand please Grandad?"

"Of course Tommy."

The carriages have names.

"Let's sit in your carriage Sophie."

They slept contentedly on the return. I cuddled Tommy and Grandma cuddled Sophie. Bliss!

'To a small child, the perfect granddad is unafraid of big dogs and fierce storms but absolutely terrified of the word "boo." Robert Brault

Epilogue

A Final 100 Words on Parenthood by Charlie Plunkett

We have come to the end of 100 little Words on Parenthood. I do hope you have enjoyed this collection of words of wisdom, wit and wonderment on all things relating to being a parent. Thank you for joining me and my lovely contributors on our journey. I'm sure many of these snippets have resounded with you and hope they have offered comfort, advice and a good giggle. As you navigate through the wonderful world of parenthood remember to take time to enjoy every magical moment and know that even the tricky bits are all part of life's rich tapestry.

Charlie x

Available now...

The True Diary of a Bride-to-be

When Charlie was little, a gypsy fortune teller at a village fair told her when she grew up she would be married twice...

Now fast forward to some thirty years later in Paris, where her boyfriend unexpectedly pops the big question.

In Charlie's diary she shares her experiences and insights as she plans for not just one wedding, but two - to the same man!

From the bright lights of Vegas to a whirlwind honeymoon around America, and back home in time for wedding number two at the beautiful Royal Pavilion in Brighton.

Her diary is a true account of exactly how she planned for each wedding without losing the plot. At the end of each week she focuses on tips and things to do to help ensure that you too will have the wedding of your dreams.

The True Diary of a Bride-to-be includes:

- Ideas on where, when and how to host the most amazing wedding.
- Little reminders to help you keep on top of managing your finances.

- Weekly guides on practicalities such as how to find the perfect people to support you on your big day.
- Finding the perfect dress and accessories.

'A fresh, funny insight into planning for a fairy-tale wedding'. **Sussex Life**

'Aimed at brides-to-be and maids looking for handy hints and a few giggles we love The True Diary of a Bride-to-be by Charlie Plunkett'. **Wedding Ideas Magazine**

'The perfect book for busy brides in need of support and entertainment'. **Your Sussex Wedding Magazine**

Also by the Author

The True Diary of a Mum-to-be a pregnancy companion

Charlie has only done two things in her life that she considers truly grown up. The first was to get married and the second was to start a family. It wasn't long before she realised how little she knew about pregnancy and birth...

Charlie's diary is an honest and funny account of her pregnancy, recounting tales of a vicious squirrel attack, a burst birth ball and numerous D.I.Y. disasters along the way.

Join Charlie as she prepares herself for the life-changing and magical experience of becoming a mum. Follow her as she travels down the sometimes bumpy road that leads to an amazing place she likes to call 'Baby Land'...

The True Diary of a Mum- to- be includes:

- A weekly guide to the changes happening in your body and how your baby is developing.
- Tips on diet, exercise and lifestyle.
- Ideas for what to include in your birth plan and how to pack a hospital/birth bag.

'Entertaining and engaging with great down to earth advice'. **Green Baby**

'If you're looking for a personal, honest, funny, warts-and-all diary of a pregnancy then this book is a must-buy!' **MumsTheWord**

'This fabulous book will be a complete hit with every mum-to-be'. **Blooming Marvellous**

'A heart-warming, personable and factual account of what to really expect when you're expecting - emotionally as well as physically!' **Hamill Baby**

Also by the Author

The True Diary of Baby's
First Year a mothering companion

In Charlie's Diary she recounts those magical first days when she finally gains access to the best club in the world 'Parenthood'... Her diary is a humorous and honest account of her attempts to be that ever elusive 'Yummy Mummy' she keeps reading about. But with boobs that are so sore getting dressed isn't really an option and no free time to visit a hairdressers, she finds that 'Scummy Mummy' may be a more accurate description of herself!

Join Charlie on her adventures in 'Baby Land' as she learns that with perseverance, love and support from her husband and those around her, she has got what it takes to be the scrumiest yummiest mummy in town!

The True Diary of Baby's First Year includes:

- Tips for regaining your figure, taking care of yourself and your baby.
- A weekly guide to your baby's development.
- Fun things to do with your baby to help with the bonding process.
- Recommended products you will utilise again and again.
- Ideas for keeping your own baby journal, photo book and time tin.

'Something different from other parenting books, an honest and thought provoking account which new parents can really feel a part of. Makes you feel OK about the tricky bits and makes you really think about the magic and joy of a new baby. A lovely, easy read to help understand what having a new baby is truly like, which leaves you smiling.' **Cuddledry**

'New and prospective mums will not be able to put this book down. A week by week guide on being a new mum - by a new mum - priceless insights and information, and full of what you really need and want to know!' **Hamill Baby**

Coming soon...

The Toddler Files

Charlie continues to chart all the milestone moments her toddler makes from his 1st birthday to his first day at school.

It is a refreshing and insightful look into the life of her adorable toddler as he progresses from 'crawling' to 'cruising' to 'walking' and 'talking' with lots of fun along the way. Not to mention teething, weaning, sleeping and sleep deprivation with the occasional tantrum thrown in for good measure...

Charlie shares her thoughts in an honest and humorous way on what it's really like living with a toddler who at times will only eat avocados and thinks that 9 pm is a good time to go to bed!

Her book is packed with tips and useful advice that helped her and is a must-buy for anyone living with a toddler.

The Toddler Files includes

- Tips for fun things to make and do with your toddler.

- Advice about all the hot topics - sleeping, teething and weaning.
- Getting the perfect balance so both your own and your child's needs are met.
- Helpful insights from other mums and dads.

Lightning Source UK Ltd.
Milton Keynes UK
UKOW040726230413

209611UK00001B/4/P